£10-95H+

LOGO Programming

SMALL COMPUTER SERIES

Consulting Editors **M. Bramer**
The Open University

J. Wilmink
University of Twente

LOGO
Programming

Peter Ross

Addison-Wesley Publishing Company
London • Reading, Massachusetts • Menlo Park, California • Amsterdam
Don Mills, Ontario • Manila • Singapore • Sydney • Tokyo

© 1983 Addison-Wesley Publishers Limited

Set by the author using **nroff,** the UNIX text-processing system, at the University of Edinburgh.

Printed in Finland by Werner Söderström Osakeyhtiö, Member of Finnprint.

Cover design by Design Expo Limited.

British Library Cataloguing In Publication Data

Ross, P.
  LOGO programming.—(Small computer series)
  1. LOGO (Computer program language)
  I. Title   II. Series
  001.64′24   QA76.73.L/

  ISBN 0-201-14637-1

  BCDEF   8987654

For Susan

Contents

ACKNOWLEDGEMENTS

The work of the LOGO group in the Department of Artificial Intelligence at the University of Edinburgh owes much to many people: Ben du Boulay, Colin McArthur, Fran Plane, Tim O'Shea, Peter Ross, Ken Johnson, Ena Inglis as well as the head of the whole enterprise Jim Howe. Others too numerous to mention have contributed significantly. This book has been influenced greatly by the work of all of these people; although it was written by one of us, all have had a hand in its origins. The Social Science Research Council has supported the LOGO work at Edinburgh for many years - this book would not have existed without their continued support of the group's work.

I would like to thank Geoff Cumming and Jim Howe for reading through the first draft of this book and making lengthy and valuable comments about its contents. My wife Susan O'Brien spent many hours correcting my spelling and style, and encouraged me at every stage - you owe her a lot!

Chapter 1
Introduction

"Clever!" said Eeyore scornfully, putting a foot
heavily on his three sticks. "Education!" said
Eeyore bitterly, jumping on his six sticks. "What
is Learning?" asked Eeyore as he kicked his twelve
sticks into the air. "A thing Rabbit knows! Ha!"

(The House at Pooh Corner, A.A.Milne)

Aims This chapter gives some background and historical information about LOGO, and tries to explain why LOGO is different
from the majority of programming languages. It also
describes the structure of the book. LOGO programming
doesn't appear until chapter 2, but you'd be well advised to
start reading this chapter first ...

1.1 PROGRAMMING AS A TOOL FOR EXPLORING IDEAS

LOGO is a computer programming language.

For some time now, it has been widely held that learning to program a computer gives you skills which are very valuable in
worlds other than that of computing. There is clearly some truth
in this; although computers work fast, they follow instructions precisely, and programming therefore requires you to be explicit and
orderly when expressing what you want the computer to do for
you. If you are not, then it does not do what you want, and
either you have to re-think your instructions to the computer or
you have to modify your goals. The habit of precise thinking that
you can learn from this can be very useful in other areas of your
life. Unfortunately, it is hard to anticipate how much you can
gain by learning to program until you embark on it and find out

for yourself. The chief question is, are the benefits worth the effort? Some of the non-technical arguments made in this chapter might help you to decide this (so keep reading).

Computers, whatever their cost or size, consist essentially of the following ingredients:

(a)   one or more processors (CPUs) which obey instructions,

(b)   some internal memory,

(c)   some external memory, such as floppy disks,

(d)   some links between what is inside the computer and what is outside, such as a keyboard, a screen, perhaps a printer or some 'paddles'.

A computer can therefore be characterised as a quantity of 'empty space' (ingredients (b) and (c)) and some restrictions on what you can do with it (ingredients (a) and (d)). Within the restrictions, only your own imagination limits what you use the empty space for. Normally, some of the empty space is given over to a set of tools, called the operating system, which makes the rest of the computer's facilities much easier to use. For example, one common task much in demand as a small part of larger tasks is that of capturing what is typed on the keyboard at appropriate moments. If you had to spell out every detail of this each time you wrote a program employing it, you might well decide to give up in disgust at the effort required. Having an operating system means that you sacrifice a little of the flexibility of the computer for the sake of being able to make it do such frequently required tasks much more easily.

This trade-off between flexibility and ease of use is also a major factor in the design of programming languages. Any language makes some kinds of tasks slightly easier and others slightly harder to express than another language; indeed, in some cases the difference is more than slight. Many of the popular programming languages now in use are 'structured'; that is, they allow you - and in fact are designed to encourage you - to chop up the task you want the machine to do, into a series of smaller sub-tasks. You can chop up the sub-tasks too, into finer and finer bits, to the point where each sub-sub-...-task is simple to explain and to program.

This decomposition of something large into smaller and more manageable parts is not peculiar to the world of programming and computers. For example, suppose you decide to repaint your living-room. You do not immediately think "I must find the car keys/get the bus" (unless neurotic about the subject), you are likely to start by thinking "I must get some paint... white, I think..." and then to go on to plan where to get it, and so on. It may be only moments, or it may be days, before you arrive at the first **action**, namely finding the car keys or finding some money, necessary to the first sub-task of getting some paint. Unfortunately, not many people make the most of this approach – you go to the shops, buy the paint and return home, and then realise you don't have a single adequate paintbrush.

The knack of tackling problems sensibly, by tackling only manageable chunks at a time and in a sensible and effective order, is one of those skills which might be more easily learned or improved through the experience of programming than by other means. In the world of programming, there are not so many of those discordant distractions (such as "I shouldn't be doing this painting, it'll be a mess, and anyway I can't afford either the time or the money"). Also, making mistakes is safe and cheap, and the computer makes it clear that there is something wrong when you have made a mistake – even if only by failing to react as expected.

There are drawbacks. A computer is immensely less tolerant than you are of leaving things unsaid. Programming languages mostly require you to be very precise about what it is you want the computer to do, and to express it in terms convenient for the machine rather than in some language which would seem adequately precise to you. For example, the following is a small fragment taken from the start of a program written in PASCAL:

```
PROGRAM ANALYSE(INPUT,OUTPUT);
VAR N, TOTAL: INTEGER;
        BUFF: PACKED ARRAY[0..511] OF CHAR;
    ........
    ........etc.
```

To write in PASCAL you must know quite a lot before you start. You need to know what punctuation is required where, what various keywords such as INPUT, VAR and INTEGER mean, when to use round brackets and when to use square brackets, and so on. If you have programmed before, you will certainly know that being careless about such things causes you considerable frustration. There are many other rules that you need to be aware of as well, rules which have no effect on the look of what you write but do concern the content. An example is that, in PASCAL on various microcomputers, quantities specified as INTEGER which you might expect to behave like everyday integers, in fact cannot be bigger than 32767. Naturally, most people who start to learn PASCAL do not think of writing programs which involve large integers. If in due course you do, surprising things happen when you run the program. Attempts to deal with integers larger than 65536 will be pointed out as faults (normally in terms drawn from computer jargon, a vast and expanding source of linguistic horrors). However, if some calculation ought to result in an integer between 32768 and 65536 then the result will actually be treated as a negative integer between -32768 and 0. If you do not know about this, it will cost you a lot of effort to find out, because it is not a fault as far as the machine is concerned.

Because normally you need considerable knowledge about the computer itself, knowledge which is not really relevant to your intentions but only to expressing them, you therefore need considerable commitment or interest when you first start to learn to program. Of necessity, you have to start with a fairly simplistic set of beliefs about what is really going on inside the computer, and have to take many things on trust or keep them at arm's length by classifying them as black magic. This is sad, because it deters many people from mastering the use of very powerful and versatile tools for intellectual exploration and enjoyment. With a computer, you can simulate nearly anything you can imagine; having a simulation, you can investigate it.

That assertion deserves some comment. Various uninformed ideas about computers still circulate, for instance

"They are only very good at dealing with numbers"

"A microcomputer is really only capable of games"

"Writing computer programs is for masochists"

The true strength of computers lies in the fact that they manipulate symbols, according to rules provided by the user. The symbols might be represented within the computer as groups of binary digits, but it is the interpretation of the symbols that matters, and that is up to the user – the computer merely obeys the rules. Suppose, for example, that you want to display Russian text on your microcomputer. You could represent the letters of the Russian alphabet as the numbers 1 to 33 and their upper case equivalents as the numbers 34 to 66. Then you could incorporate various rules within a program, such as

-        If key 'A' is pressed, store the number 1 (so key 'A' corresponds to the first letter of the Russian alphabet). If key 'B' is pressed, store the number 2. ...etc.

- To convert all lower case Russian letters to upper case, look at each number. If it is between 1 and 33, then add 33 to it.

- To display the letter corresponding to 1, put dots on the screen at the following (X,Y) co-ordinates and move the origin of co-ordinates so that the next character displayed will be in a sensible place (for example, just to the right of the last one).

These rules are purely to do with numbers, but they could be incorporated into a word processing system for Russian text. The trick of computer programming is to devise rules which operate on numbers, as the computer knows them, such that the content of the rules is consistent with the interpretation you want to put on them. Usually the rules are not as straightforward as these examples suggest. Besides deciding to represent Russian letters as the numbers 1 to 33, you would also have to decide how to represent words, sentences and paragraphs – probably by deciding how to organise sets of representations of letters. One of the important points in the later part of this book will be to do with choosing how to represent what is to be modelled; the choice has a big influence on how easy it is to specify the rules.

Having chosen representations for the ingredients of what you want to model, and thought a little about the rules, the main task is to translate it all into one or more computer programs. Certain maxims are worth remembering at this point. One is that it is better to try to be as general as possible – that way you eventually build yourself a toolkit, and your programming gets easier and faster. Another is that it is better to break the whole task into small bits – they are easier to play about with and to modify. These and many others will be illustrated in this book.

LOGO was designed to avoid most of the initial hurdles in learning to program, and yet to be very powerful. In particular, you need know nothing about the guts of your computer before you start, and you can get interesting results for your efforts almost at once. After all, the whole point of using a computer is to make interesting things happen on your terminal or elsewhere outside the machine. In short, LOGO offers the power in modelling and expression which might be found in other languages, yet avoids much of the bureaucracy and specialised computer science that other languages demand. It is **not** intended to be the ultimate in programming. In general, what can be done in one language can be done in any other, perhaps more awkwardly and perhaps more simply.

1.2 SOME HISTORY

LOGO was designed at Bolt Beranek and Newman Inc in Cambridge, Massachusetts, in the late 1960s and so is younger than most other languages. It was created as part of an experiment to test the idea that programming might be a useful educational discipline to teach children. The first research project was closely related to mathematics and the ideas it sought to test were, roughly, these:

-   Programming might be the basis for a useful language, not directly linked to computing, in which to talk about problem-solving divorced from the background of any particular school subject.

-   Programming might be a good vehicle for illustrating some mathematical concepts which are normally hard to grasp.

-   A computer, with the right programming language, could be a wonderful 'mathematical laboratory' in which it would be possible to experiment with abstract ideas it would otherwise be hard to give form to.

The word 'mathematics' being taken in a very wide sense, is the art of being able to analyse and explore rules governing physical or imaginary but logical worlds. The original version of LOGO was designed by Wallace Feurzeig, Daniel Bobrow and Seymour Papert[1] – their design owed much to another language called LISP[1], now widely used for research in Artificial Intelligence. LOGO was refined at the Artificial Intelligence Laboratory of M.I.T. and at the Department of Artificial Intelligence of the University of Edinburgh, Scotland.

At first LOGO had no provision for computer graphics, the necessary hardware being prohibitively expensive in those days for an education project. Then, fairly early on, graphics were incorporated into the language, in the form of 'turtle graphics'. This

1 LISP is powerful (it was invented in the mid-1960s (at M.I.T. (who still use it for A.I. research (as do many others (though less so in Europe (where Prolog is a strong rival language))))) and has been much developed since) but tends to be almost unreadable (because its syntax depends so much on parentheses)!

is now such a major facet of LOGO for beginners that many people mistakenly assume that 'turtle graphics' is the whole of LOGO.

Graphics have probably contributed most to the success of LOGO. Producing pictures is tremendously appealing, and offers enormous scope for experimenting. Many other programming languages treat graphics as an extra, 'bolted on' afterwards. Although they offer sophisticated ways of generating pictures, it needs a sophisticated user to understand and use their graphics-related parts. For example, they nearly all assume a fair familiarity with Cartesian co-ordinates; this would make them inaccessible to a child who had not yet met them in school. LOGO's 'turtle graphics' avoids such traps, by providing a very simple means of picture construction which demands no prior investment in mathematical or computer knowledge. The essential knowledge is merely an awareness of familiar concepts such as 'forward', 'backward', 'left' and 'right'. This makes it possible for children, even young ones, to start using LOGO.

Various versions of LOGO appeared in the course of time. Most American versions are recognisable as dialects of the M.I.T. LOGO, although the version available for the Texas Instruments TI 99/4 is somewhat unusual compared to others such as Apple LOGO and Terrapin LOGO. Nevertheless, it too sprang from an M.I.T. research project. An assumption underlying the work that went into these versions was that LOGO would never easily fit into the conventional maths curriculum – the curriculum would eventually change to incorporate what LOGO had to offer. In the U.K. a different dialect of LOGO evolved from research work done at the Department of Artificial Intelligence of the University of Edinburgh from 1972 onwards. This was based on the belief that LOGO would best gain acceptance by being used within the conventional curriculum in some way – evolution rather than revolution, so to speak. Thus Edinburgh LOGO was developed, through various research projects, to be even less demanding on the user's understanding and prior knowledge than the M.I.T. versions. A microcomputer version of Edinburgh LOGO exists for the 380Z and 480Z (Z80 based machines running CP/M) produced by Research Machines Ltd. of Oxford, one of the largest suppliers of microcomputers to British schools.

All the educational research carried out so far suggests that LOGO has a great deal to offer as a means of teaching conceptual thinking, but no survey yet has been on a big enough scale to be conclusive. You may wonder, if it seems to be such a good thing, why it did not become available to the public much sooner than it did? The main reason is this: LOGO requires more from a computer than most other popular languages do. Until the

1980s, a computer powerful enough to provide what LOGO demands would have been too expensive to be a commercial success.

1.3 A DIGRESSION ABOUT ARTIFICIAL INTELLIGENCE (A.I.)

(You can safely skip this section if you want.)

At first sight it might seem strange that educational research should be done in the world of Artificial Intelligence – a Department of Education, or some such body, might seem more the appropriate place for LOGO. To understand the reasons for this you need to know a little about what Artificial Intelligence is and what it aims to do. It is sometimes defined as the use of computers to study intelligence and, in particular, human thought. The definition does not convey much.

To get a little feel for the subject, consider the following example of the sort of unrealistic 'intelligence test' that often appears in the newspapers:

Which is the odd one out?

When first confronted with such a problem, various ideas spring to mind immediately. Perhaps the 'Y' is the odd one out, because it is the only one which has pretensions to being a vowel. Perhaps it is a code – if you try the usual trick of substituting 1 for 'A', 2 for 'B' etc., then it turns out that 'Y' is the only odd number, so it really is the 'odd one out'. At some point you might make the leap of looking at them as geometric figures rather than as letters of the alphabet. In that case you might realise that the 'Z' qualifies as odd one out because it is made up of three straight lines rather than two, or perhaps because it involves two line junctions rather than one. The more you look, the more justifications you can find for any particular one being the answer.

Now imagine that you had to write a computer program to mimic your solution of the problem. The work you would have to put in before starting to write such a program could well be called Artificial Intelligence (if you did a good job of it). You would, amongst other problems, have to figure out why you made the leap from considering letters to considering shapes, and why you did it when you did. Had you worked through all the letter possibilities? No, there is a huge number of them and you could not possibly try them all. Some obnoxious whiz-kid, for instance, might have been able to claim that the 'V' was the odd one out because all the others were initials of authors of children's books published in 1912! You presumably made the leap because you felt that you were starting to look for possibilities that were too unlikely. But ... how do you embody the notion of 'too unlikely' in a computer program? Moreover, how do you encapsulate the knowledge and experience that made you plump for the attribute of shape as a likely factor to explore?

The reason that computers are so vital to the subject of Artificial Intelligence is that you cannot get away with hand-waving about these points in such problems. The computer only obeys instructions; it cannot decide for itself to switch to some new tack, even if the program to explore that new tack exists. The program which mimics your solution to the above problem – do not try writing one, it's a huge can of worms – would have to include regular checks about the likelihood of success with the current approach. Likelihood is not easy to quantify – it depends on past experience. A good program would have to be capable of resuming the exploration of a previously rejected avenue if it begins to look more promising after all, as others grow less likely.

The absolute lack of intelligence on the part of a computer makes the act of writing a program to model something a good test of a theory in A.I. The problem above is not representative of work in the field – current research (1983) is concerned with more fundamental questions which this problem only hints at. It should help you appreciate, however, that the world of A.I. has had good reason to spend a lot of effort in developing computer languages specifically for modelling purposes. Those now used in A.I., such as LISP and PROLOG, are geared to bring out the aspects of computer programming which are most useful in model-ling and to play down those aspects which would be least relevant to the aims of the subject. LOGO is one product of that effort; as such, it is a remarkable success.

The studying of how and what people learn through using LOGO also fits in with the interests of workers in A.I.

1.4 ABOUT THIS BOOK

What it is not

This book is not a programming manual in the normal sense. It does not aim purely to teach you how to read and write LOGO – other manuals[1] already do that well. It is not much concerned with the technical aspects of computers. If you want to know why smoke is coming from your Apple II, how to make it control your coffee grinder, or why the disk drive is making that grating noise, then look elsewhere...

What it is

On first learning to program a computer, most people estimate their own abilities very badly. Either they plough through a manual or a course and then immediately embark on trying to write a program which will play a decent game of chess, or they find themselves short of inspiration and confidence and rapidly lose interest. Either way, the machine fails to live up to their expectations. Often the problem is that only a hazy distinction is made between knowing the mechanics of programming and knowing how to put it to use.

The purpose of this book is to help you develop the knowledge and experience to be able to make the most of LOGO as a tool. True, to do so involves teaching you to program in LOGO. However, there is a widespread view that good programming is the private preserve of geniuses, that mere mortals cannot aspire to great results, and that a measure of the worth of a program is the amount of ingenuity which went into it. This book should help to demolish that idea. The power to express your ideas well and to develop them thoroughly is **not** a gift – it is something which can be learned, and LOGO makes it enjoyable.

1.5 THOUGHTS FOR TEACHERS

(You can skip this section too if you are never going to find yourself teaching others about LOGO, even informally.)

Much has been said in magazines and journals about the educational value of LOGO. Not much has been said about the problems. One of the major snags is that, while students can

---

1 For example, 'LOGO' by Harold Abelson, pub. by Byte/McGraw-Hill Publications, 1982, or 'Apple LOGO', by the same author and publisher, 1982.

learn a lot from making mistakes and tracking them down, it is extremely disenchanting to make too many mistakes and too little progress towards becoming fluent in the use of LOGO. Your problem is to leave a student alone long enough to develop confidence in his ideas, and yet be aware enough to spot when help is necessary. There are asides throughout the book which point out areas of likely trouble.

An aside – apologies now and hereafter to readers who are women – sexist sympathies are not intended by references to 'he' and 'his', but this book aims to be short and readable. Indeed, you may care to ponder why girls did significantly better than boys in a high school project were LOGO was used to teach the traditional mathematics syllabus.

As a teacher, even if you are not one in the formal sense, you ought to bear one or two points in mind. A beginner is going to have his own ideas about what is really going on inside the computer as he works with LOGO. Usually this is a very simplified version of the truth, but it has the great benefit of making the whole system seem manageable. The habit of simplification is not only used by beginners, of course – for example, just about everyone characterises their government as a sort of collective being with a rather dumb mind of its own. Doing so makes it seem comprehensible.

Such simplification can be useful or it can be obstructive. It is useful only if it helps you to grasp why things are happening and permits you to predict what will happen in response to your actions. A significant part of the art of teaching consists of encouraging pupils to adopt some simplifying and familiar analogy, and then getting them to modify and enlarge it in a reasonably consistent way to take account of new and previously inexplicable details. What has been said above might lead you to think that, in the world of LOGO, this is going to be easier than usual. It is to some extent, but do not imagine you can be complacent about it – being easier does not mean that it is easy. To put you in the mood, consider how you might tackle these two questions from a bright but beginning LOGO user:

"How can the computer read what is engraved on the keys? If I press 'F' then an F appears on the screen, but the computer has no eyes."

"If I type a lot, or press RETURN many times, then some of what I have typed goes off the top of the screen. Can I get it back? (Note: the answer is no) and where did it go?"

If you are going to be using LOGO in formal classroom teaching, you will need to do some careful planning. Yes, LOGO can be a vehicle for teaching programming, though there seems little point in teaching programming for its own sake. After all, while LOGO is a powerful and relatively simple language, it is representative of only one of various classes of programming languages, each of which has its own underlying 'programming concepts'. It is the particular approach to expressing ideas which is valuable in LOGO, rather than the computer science aspects.

If you want to use LOGO as a means for teaching topics in some subject such as mathematics or geography (where you could use it for training people in ideas about graphic representations), then you will need a good deal of organised material. This is true no matter what programming language is used. You will also have to figure out how to teach the necesary LOGO programming **before** getting your pupils to put that knowledge to use in experimenting with your subject.

One neglected approach is to use LOGO to underpin a group discussion. You can do this even if you only have one machine per class, by making the machine the arbiter of who is right and who is wrong in the discussion or by getting the group to plan how to model something, with you as the typist.

Finally – for the moment – do not be put off by articles[1] which try to lay down the law about how LOGO should be used. If it suits you to devise LOGO programs which others will use but need not understand, because it is an easy language in which to express your intentions, then go ahead.

1.6 THE LAYOUT OF THE BOOK

As you will have seen, sections within chapters are numbered. The numbering is hierarchical – section 2.6.1 is subsection 1 of section 6 of chapter 2. Figures are also numbered by chapter – figure 2.3 is figure 3 of chapter 2. This makes it easier to refer to them, especially because figures might not always appear on the same page on which they are first mentioned in the text. Chunks of LOGO look like this:

```
PRINT 654 * 321
```

You will find that long lines on the Apple II's screen look odd – the screen is only wide enough for 40 characters and if you type off the end of one line the machine continues for you on the

---

1 Or even this book.

next line. This may cause a word to be split in the middle if it starts close to the end of a line. Long lines of LOGO will be indicated in this book by indenting the continuation. The following example is not LOGO, but you could type it nevertheless (the LOGO system will merely object to it). There are only two lines; you could make it appear on your screen very much as it appears here by the simple step of inserting extra spaces between certain of the words:

```
THIS IS NOT LOGO, JUST AN EXAMPLE OF HOW
       ONE VERY LONG LINE OF TYPING WILL BE
       SHOWN IN THE TEXT OF THIS BOOK.
THIS IS A SECOND LINE.
```

Diagrams appear as shown in figure 1.1. The box around it shows where the useful edges of the screen are, so that you can get an idea of what it ought to look like on your computer. The box will not appear on your screen (unless you add it yourself), as it is an extra included when this book was printed so that you can judge the scale — which is useful if you want to try marrying two

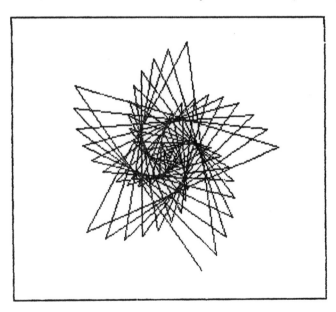

Figure 1.1

or more diagrams.

Appendices describe various versions of LOGO which existed at the time the book was published. They are worth looking at even if you have no chance to use another version; the variations in what they provide might give you some useful ideas about general LOGO commands you can create for yourself.

There are exercises. Those that have a reasonably short and instructive solution are answered at the back of the book. They are **not** meant to be a graded series to take you through everything that needs to be practised. Try them as you encounter them or you'll be missing a lot.

Chapter 2
Turtle graphics

"It just shows what can be done by taking a little trouble," said Eeyore. "Do you see, Pooh? Do you see, Piglet? Brains first and then Hard Work. Look at it! That's the way to build a house," said Eeyore proudly.

(The House at Pooh Corner, A.A.Milne)

Aims   This chapter has two purposes. One is to introduce you to the LOGO drawing commands. They are, individually, remarkably simple; using them with a few of the more generally useful features of LOGO also introduced in this chapter should equip you to produce some fairly elaborate drawings. The other purpose is more general: to show LOGO as an interesting tool for experiment and investigation.

NOTE   There are examples of LOGO throughout this book. The version of LOGO on which they are based is one marketed by Terrapin Inc. of Boston and by Krell Inc. of New York, for the Apple II microcomputer. It will be referred to in the text as Terrapin LOGO. If you have some other version of LOGO, you will not be able to copy the examples unthinkingly, even though there are more similarities than differences between the various LOGOs that exist. You should treat the examples of LOGO as prototypes of ideas – even if it is this LOGO you have! Anything without a ready counterpart in Apple LOGO or TI LOGO will be indicated in the text. Radio Shack Color LOGO has so many differences that you should not rely on any of the information given in the body of the book; an Appendix describes it.

2.1 **INTRODUCTION**

Suppose that you have just switched on your microcomputer and got LOGO going – if you do not know how, look at the instructions that came with the disk. On the screen you should see, amongst other things, a small solid rectangle, the **cursor**, which will be just to the right of the **prompt**; in Terrapin LOGO this is

?

– on a few other micros it is

W:

(the initial W is for 'Waiting'). This prompt indicates that LOGO is waiting for you to type in a command of some sort. If you have not done so already, try typing a few letters of the alphabet to see what happens, then press the RETURN key. Pressing the RETURN key indicates to LOGO that what you have typed is (perhaps) a command that you want obeyed. Unless you were lucky in your choice of letters, LOGO will print an error message on the screen, the gist of which will be that your command is not a known one. There are two points to make here:

-        LOGO errors may cost you some time, but they do not damage anything you spent money on.

-        Making errors is, as in other subjects, one of the best ways to learn things. It's the normal thing to be doing, rather than the exception!

Initially LOGO will only recognise around a hundred commands. However, one of the beauties of the language is that you can extend the set of commands it knows about – this is the main topic of the chapter after this. Between 10% and 20% of the commands available at the start are to do with drawing. These are introduced in this chapter.

2.2 **THE BASIC TURTLE GRAPHICS COMMANDS**

Each time you start LOGO up, you should see a short introductory message, and the prompt. Type

DRAW

and press RETURN. Even DRAW is not needed with some versions of LOGO. You should now see an arrowhead in the middle of the screen. On the Apple II it points upward. The arrowhead is called the turtle; there are commands that change its location, others that change its direction and one or two that do both. A useful characterisation of it, especially for children, is

"an animal which crawls across a sheet of paper, towing a pencil or an eraser"

and the screen can be characterised as

"a sheet of paper which you are looking down on from above"

Initially the turtle will draw a line as it moves.

The fundamental commands which control the turtle are FORWARD, BACK, LEFT and RIGHT, and each requires you to supply a number indicating 'how much'. The number gives degrees of rotation (360 is a full turn on the spot) for LEFT and RIGHT, and 'turtle units' for FORWARD and BACK. For example, try typing

FORWARD 50

(do not forget to press RETURN as well). The turtle will move forward 50 units, drawing a line. One 'turtle unit' does not correspond to some number of inches or centimeters - the physical length of the line depends on the size of your screen. However, the screen has a fixed size when measured in terms of 'turtle units'. If you now type the additional commands

RIGHT 120
FORWARD 50
RIGHT 120
FORWARD 50

then your drawing should look like figure 2.1. If you are puzzled by why it should be RIGHT 120 rather than, say, RIGHT 60 then try the commands with RIGHT 60 instead and see what happens - experiment! There are commands for cleaning off the drawing and returning the turtle to where it was (and facing upward) at the start - in Terrapin LOGO they are

HOME
CLEARSCREEN

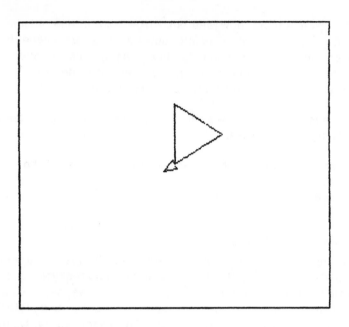

Figure 2.1

2.3 SOME TERMINOLOGY

There is some terminology which it is sensible to mention here. Things like CLEAN and FORWARD and so on are called **procedures**; a command is really an instruction to LOGO to **execute** (that is, obey) some procedure(s). It is not vital for you to make a distinction between 'command' and 'procedure' – you should just be aware of the terminology at the moment.

You may note that, although you must supply a number for FORWARD (what happens if you do not?), you supply nothing else with HOME (what happens if you do?). The customary way of describing this is to say that

FORWARD takes one input, which must be a number

but

HOME takes no input

There are other procedures that take more than one input, and even some for which the number of inputs can be unknown. Examples of these will appear in chapters 3 and 4.

Try the command

RANDOM 50

– you will get an error message pointing out that you have not said what to do with some random number less than 50. This is because RANDOM not only requires one input – in the command it was 50 – it also produces an **output**. RANDOM's output is a random positive integer less than the input number. The output number can be used wherever a number input would be acceptable:

FORWARD RANDOM 50

would move the turtle forward by a random integer number of turtle units less than 50. FORWARD needs a number for its input, RANDOM 50 outputs a number – if you like, you can choose to think that the expression RANDOM 50 **is** a number.

The procedures FORWARD, BACK, LEFT, RIGHT, HOME and CLEARSCREEN (and many others) do not produce an output, they merely have some effect. It is one of the fundamental rules about LOGO commands that if something produces an output, it must be used as the input to something else – you cannot leave outputs lying about unused.

2.4 DRAWINGS

There are abbreviations for the most commonly used procedures, to spare your fingertips. In particular, you can use

FD for FORWARD
BK for BACK
LT for LEFT
RT for RIGHT
CS for CLEARSCREEN

EXERCISES

There are various things you could now take time to investigate:

(1)   What happens when the turtle reaches the edge of the screen?

(2)   What are the dimensions of the screen in 'turtle units'?

(3)   How much should the turtle be turned from its initial heading so that it points at a corner of the screen (trial and error is the method, unless you want to indulge in trigonometry)?

(4)   Do FD, BK, LT and RT accept negative numbers, and if so what is the effect?

(5)   Do those commands accept numbers with decimal parts, or do they just ignore any decimal part? This requires forethought – the decimal part certainly gets ignored when showing lines on the screen; the question is, is the turtle really where it seems to be or is it a fraction of a turtle unit further along the line?

The answers to each of these might be useful to you later on.

You will find, in Terrapin LOGO, the answer to question (1) is that the turtle reappears at the opposite edge of the screen when it moves off any edge. This is called **wrapping**; you can prevent it happening in subsequent commands by using the command

     NOWRAP

and you can switch back to having the turtle wrap by using

     WRAP

When the turtle is allowed to wrap, try the commands

     CS
     RT 50
     FD 30000

in order to see what happens when you send the turtle forward some distance that is much larger than the dimensions of the screen. There is nothing remarkable about the angle 50 in this trio - try some others (some choices are remarkable).

EXERCISES

You might also like to try your hand at constructing some simple drawings, such as

(6a)   some simple polygons - essentially sets of paired FOR-
        WARD and RIGHT (or LEFT) commands

(6b)   something less regular, such as a drawing of your micro-
        computer. Keep it fairly simple, unless you are a maso-
        chist. Planning the drawing should remind you of those
        popular challenges 'draw this without lifting pen from
        paper...'

At this point you might think, with reason, that LOGO drawings require you to type too many commands for fairly simple
results. If more complex drawings were going to be correspond-
ingly more arduous to construct, you would be justified in aban-
doning the whole enterprise immediately. However, as you might
expect - and you ought to have expected that the designers of
LOGO would have thought of it - there are ways of making things
easier. You can combine several commands into one, by merely
putting one after another with space between. For example,

    HOME CS

is one command formed from two. Similarly,

    FD 50 RT 120

is one (compound) command, and three such commands in
sequence will draw an equilateral triangle. This allows you to make
up single commands which are very long; if they spread to the
point where they are going to overflow the right-hand edge of the
screen, do not worry - just keep typing and what you type will
appear on the next line down. DON'T press RETURN when your
typing reaches the right-hand edge unless you want LOGO to obey
the command you've typed so far. So, when drawing a square,
part of your screen might look like this

? FD 50 RT 90 FD 50 RT 90 FD 50 RT 90 FD
50 RT 90

and LOGO will treat the whole thing as one command. There is a limit to how long a line can be – it is roughly six complete widths of the screen.

What you can do about typing mistakes depends on which version of LOGO you have. In Terrapin LOGO on the Apple II you can use the ESC key to rub out characters and use the arrow keys to move the cursor back and forward in the line, to allow you to pick what you want to rub out. Putting the cursor in the middle of the line somewhere and then typing, causes what is to the right to be pushed to the right. Two other options are very useful, but are slightly less convenient because they require you to press the key marked CTRL, and to press another while holding it down (the CTRL key is similar to the SHIFT keys in its use). The options are

CTRL-D (that is, CTRL and D) which is very like ESC. ESC deletes the character just to the left of the cursor, CTRL-D deletes the character which is underneath the cursor

CTRL-K (that is, CTRL and K) which deletes everything from where the cursor is to the end of the command.

There is a variety of other things you can do, but these are the most useful possibilities. Consult the manual that came with your LOGO system to see what powers you can call on for correcting typing – the repertoire may even be amended by the supplier from time to time, so it will not be described in this book.

LOGO has a number of commands which are useful in many situations. One is for those occasions when repetition of some command (perhaps compound) is required:

REPEAT 5 [FD 50 RT 72]

is an example that draws a pentagon. The square brackets are necessary here. Unfortunately the square brackets characters are not visibly engraved anywhere on the Apple II keyboard. To type them:

[is shift-M (i.e. hold down one of the two shift keys and while holding it down, press M.

] is shift-N.

If you are prone to forgetting this kind of detail, get some very small sticky labels, write the symbols on them and affix them to the keys or to the Apple case.

The general form of the REPEAT command is

REPEAT number [command]

and, using it, you should now be able to draw any regular polygon. It is a very powerful command, more so than might appear at first sight. Think of it as a command with another command inside it – then you should see that this is legal LOGO, and it will produce an interesting pattern, shown in figure 2.2.

REPEAT 10 [RT 36 REPEAT 5 [FD 40
    RT 72]]

This gives you a prototype for all sorts of 'rotated polygon' patterns. There are several noteworthy points about it:

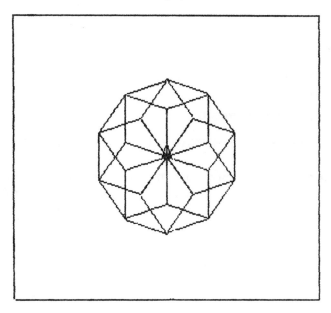

Figure 2.2

-   The REPEAT command on the inside just draws one pen-
    tagon, and leaves the turtle as it was before. Such a
    command, that afterwards has affected neither the turtle's
    location nor its heading, is sometimes referred to as
    'state-transparent'. The turtle's location and heading are
    together known as the turtle's state.

-   The main REPEAT command is thus something of the form

        REPEAT 10 [RT 36 state-transparent command]

    so that the turtle will in effect have turned by 10x36 =
    360 degrees by the end. Thus the whole command is also
    state-transparent.

-   those numbers 10 and 36 give a pleasingly regular and
    state-transparent result because they multiply to give 360.
    How about trying pairs of numbers that multiply to give
    720, or some other multiple of 360? For example,

        REPEAT 5 [RT 144 ...]

    Some are not worth the effort:

        REPEAT 12 [RT 60 ...]

    is just the equivalent of

        REPEAT 2 [REPEAT 6 [RT 60 ...]]

    and so you would just be repeating a state-transparent
    procedure twice. Doing that means nothing more than
    retracing the drawing, because just before the second
    time, the turtle will be as it was just before the first time.
    A little thought, and perhaps some experiment, should
    show you how to spot which pairs of numbers are poten-
    tially interesting, and which are not.

-   The idea of polygons rotated about one spot may come to
    seem limited after you've tried a few. A variation that
    offers further possibilities is

        REPEAT x [FD y RT z state-transparent command]

    since this too is state-transparent if the numbers x and z
    are suitably chosen. The drawings in figures 2.3 and 2.4

were produced by such a command[1].

All the drawings produced by one such command have a somewhat sterile regularity about them. It should be reasonably clear that this is because in any REPEAT command like those above, the only thing that changes from one repetition to the next is the state of the turtle - its position or heading or both. What the turtle actually does at each repetition is unchanging, and that is because the numbers - distances or angles - are unvarying. There are some exciting variations on this theme. The first is just to make the command even more elaborate. There comes a point at which there are so many different sorts of regularity in a picture that it is difficult for the eye to grasp what the subsections of the pattern are that have been repeated. Consider the following hypothesis:

It is the state-transparent parts that catch the attention.

The idea of studying such a subjective hypothesis may surprise you if you are of a scientific turn of mind. Nevertheless, you may or may not agree with this, but you can investigate it by trying various sorts of REPEAT combinations (as one or as several commands) where there are several state-transparent ingredients, and various in which there are only one or two at most. The drawing in figure 2.5 is state-transparent, with only one state-transparent ingredient within it. The command was

```
REPEAT 12 [ FD 30 REPEAT 4 [ FD 15
RT 90 ] BK 30 RT 30 ]
```

Try experimenting. Get some other people's opinions too - the results may not be as subjective as you think.

Another of the possibilities for variety is to have the turtle erase some parts of a drawing, or to have it not draw at all for some parts. In Terrapin LOGO the turtle cannot erase directly, it can only overwrite something previously drawn with a new line in the same colour as the background (so it looks like erasure is happening, to all intents and purposes). There are two useful commands: PENCOLOR (or PC for short) which takes an input

---

1 Warning for TI LOGO users: the TI 99/4 and TI 99/4a machines have a limitation on their conventional graphics abilities. You know about it when you get the message OUT OF INK, and the only thing to do is to clear the screen and start over. Try the rotated pentagon command given earlier, with FD 50 instead of FD 40, to see this. You may have to scale down some of the commands used as illustrations in this book, in order to avoid the limitation. In compensation, TI LOGO offers some very powerful animation features.

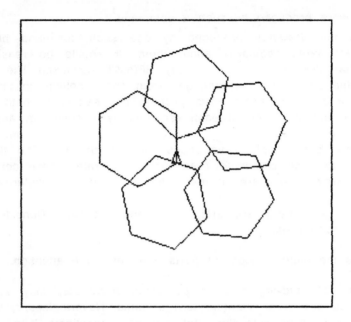

Figure 2.3

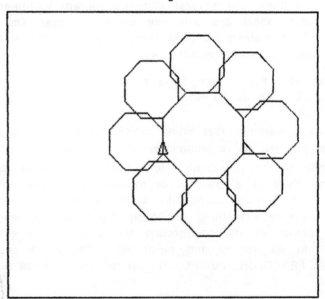

Figure 2.4

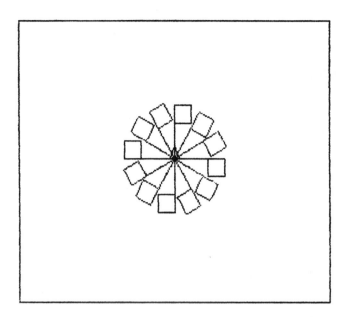

Figure 2.5

which must be a number between 0 and 6 and makes the turtle draw in the corresponding colour in future, and BACKGROUND (or BG for short) which also expects a number between 0 and 6 and sets the colour of the background. Colour 6 is curious; it is an "inverting" colour which causes others to change to their reverse. What that means, and what colours 0 to 5 are, is something you can best find out for yourself by trying PC and BG – they depend on the sort of display you have, although they should work (if only to make a feeble difference) even on a black and white display. That is why they are numbers rather than names such as 'green' and 'violet' – such is the standardisation in video technology that what looks green on one display may well look violet on another!

On the Apple II the initial settings are 0 for the background and 1 for the turtle's pen colour. Provided you do not change the background colour, therefore, the way to make the turtle erase is to give the command

PENCOLOR 0

and the way to make it not draw or erase at all is to use the command

PENUP

or PU for short. You can make it resume drawing (with the current pen colour) by the command

PENDOWN

or PD for short. Try these in a compound command, for example

FD 100 PENCOLOR 0 BK 50 PENUP BK 50

should leave the turtle at its starting point, with a 50-unit line in front of it. You need to give the command

PENCOLOR 1

to get the turtle to resume drawing when it moves.

You can greatly extend the potential for drawings by using variables instead of explicit numbers. This idea is so important throughout the rest of the book that it deserves a section to itself.

2.5 VARIABLES

The MAKE command

MAKE "Z 50

gives a variable[1] named Z the value 50 (note the quote mark just before the Z). The name of the variable does not have to be a single letter, it can be anything, such as HIPPOPOTAMUS or HYPOTENUSE, which you find appropriate and not uncomfortably long. You can use any characters apart from the left and right square brackets and spaces; LENGTH.OF.SIDE is a perfectly good name for a variable.

Then you can use a command such as

FORWARD :Z

to move the turtle forward 50. Note the colon (':'), it means 'the value of the variable called'.

---

1 WHAT, you were not very sure about variables in your early days of algebra? The image to keep in mind, then, is this: think of all the numbers, negative or positive, stretching in an orderly line way off into the distance (like railway tracks). Imagine a large luggage label with the name Z written on it, hanging on one of the numbers, 50 for instance. Then you can refer to 50 by the name on the label, rather than as '50'. Moreover, you can move the label around from number to number as the occasion demands. You can also have several labels on one number. Solving algebraic equations is just a matter of deducing which number some label is hanging on...

Digression

People often ask two questions about the MAKE command. The first is, what is that quote mark doing there? To answer, consider the command MAKE FORWARD 50. Does this give a variable named FORWARD the value 50, or is it a mangled attempt to move the turtle? The quote mark prevents LOGO mistaking the name as a command – and remember, it was mentioned that in LOGO the user can create new commands (and perhaps create one called Z). To be more precise, the quote mark signifies that what follows is just a word and nothing more than that. Chapter 4 explains various LOGO commands which are concerned with words rather than specifically with numbers. You can PRINT a word by

    PRINT "HELLO

All you need to remember at present is that MAKE expects its first input to be a word, and it takes the word to be the name of a variable. The second input could also be a word if you wanted:

    MAKE "CLEOPATRA "EGYPT
    PRINT :CLEOPATRA

will print EGYPT.

The second question is, why is there no matching quote at the end of a word? The answer is that LOGO takes the space after the name to mark the end of the name; it would be wasting your time to force you to put in something which is really superfluous. In Terrapin LOGO, a quote mark at the end, or within a name, will just be taken as part of the name.

Digression for those familiar with another language:

LOGO is unusually friendly about variables. You do not have to declare the name or type of variables beforehand, as you would in PASCAL for instance. MAKE looks for a variable of the given name; if there is not one, it creates one. Moreover, the type is the type of the current value.

In most LOGO systems, there is another way to get at the value of a variable. In Terrapin LOGO there is a procedure called THING which expects one input, a word naming a variable, and returns the value of the variable called by that name. For instance, if the variable called Z has the value 50, then

FORWARD THING "Z

will send the turtle forward 50. Again, the quote mark in that command exists to let the LOGO system know that the Z is merely a name rather than the name of a procedure that it should run.

It might seem that the colon is nothing more than an abbreviation for THING. In fact, it is something even less than that. To illustrate the problem, consider this sequence of LOGO commands:

MAKE "FRED 50
MAKE "X "FRED
FORWARD THING THING "X

The second command gave the variable called X a value – the value was just a bit of text, namely the word FRED. The FORWARD command is equivalent to

FORWARD THING "FRED

which is equivalent to

FORWARD 50

However, the following is NOT the same:

FORWARD ::FRED

This command would send LOGO looking for a variable called by the name :FRED, but the colon is NOT a procedure (there would need to be a space between the colon and what followed it if it were a procedure). You could always make a variable whose name was :FRED, by

MAKE ":FRED 35

but your FORWARD command would move the turtle 35 units rather than 50. The colon is only a sort of notational convenience rather than a procedure; however, it is so convenient that the procedure THING only gets used where the colon would not do the job, such as in the example above.

2.6 ARITHMETIC

Introducing the standard arithmetic operations of addition, subtraction, multiplication and division together with MAKE considerably expands the potential for drawings. For instance, the command

```
MAKE "Z :Z + 2
```

gives Z a new value 2 bigger than it previously had. This deserves some comment. The command is still something of the general form

```
MAKE "Z number
```

but the number is :Z + 2 rather than something explicit. In LOGO, as in real life, the '+' adds two numbers together. It produces an **output**, also a number, that is the sum of the two numbers; such an expression is acceptable wherever a number is acceptable. The same applies to other LOGO arithmetic procedures: '*' for multiplication, '/' for division and '-' for subtraction. You should now be in a position to understand that a command such as

```
MAKE "Z 3
REPEAT 50 [ FD :Z RT 90 MAKE "Z :Z + 2 ]
```

will draw a sort of rectangular spiral.

EXERCISES

Here are various things it would be worth taking some time to investigate:

(7)   Nothing has been said about the layout of commands. Where are spaces necessary, for instance? Experiment — nothing worse than an error message will happen. You will remember better if you figure it out than if you clutter up your mental imagery by turning to the manual at this point.

(8)   The MAKE command allows you to alter the sizes of distances and angles between repetitions. Try some variants of REPEAT commands you tried before. (This might show you that it's a good idea to keep notes of your successes.)

(9)   How do the arithmetic procedures behave when some of the numbers are negative?

---

(10)   What happens when you try to divide a number by zero, or try to multiply numbers together to get some colossal result?

Spend some time playing with the arithmetic procedures. The simple way to do this is to use the procedure PRINT – its single input can be also be a number:

    MAKE "NUM 5
    PRINT :NUM * 5

will print 25. Try predicting what the commands

    PRINT 3 * 4 + 5 * 6

    PRINT 12/4/2

    PRINT −4 + 5*6

    PRINT 6/2+4

will print, then try them. In Terrapin LOGO at least, complicated arithmetic expressions are worked out according to the following rules:

(i)   all the multiplications and divisions are done first (so 3*4+5*6 is really 12+30 rather than 3*9*6)

(ii)   then all the additions and subtractions are done

(iii)   whenever rules (i) and (ii) are ambiguous, work left-to-right (so 6/3*7 is 2*7 rather 6/21)

(iv)   parentheses can be used in the obvious ways.

BEWARE of subtraction – it is easy to get confused between (a) subtracting one number from another, and (b) using a negative number, because the minus sign is used for both purposes. The command

    PRINT 5 −2

does not print 3. It prints 5 and then LOGO complains that you have not said what to do with −2. The safe course is to put a

space after the minus sign unless you mean to indicate a negative number.

PRINT 5 - 2

will print 3.

There are still further possibilities for confusion:

PRINT RANDOM 10 + 12

is the same as

PRINT RANDOM 22

and different from

PRINT (RANDOM 10) + 12

The rule is that LOGO does all the '+', '*', '-' and '/' it can
before anything else.

To be absolutely safe, use parentheses to make your meaning clear.

PRINT RANDOM (10+12)
PRINT RANDOM (10   +12)
PRINT RANDOM (10+   12)
PRINT RANDOM (10+12   )

are all the same, and the effort of including the parentheses is
only a small price to pay for avoiding arithmetic boobytraps.

2.6.1 Large Numbers

Investigate how large and how small a number your LOGO system
will let you work with. In Terrapin LOGO numbers with more than
about six significant digits get printed in a specialised form, and it
will also recognise numbers given by you in this form:

1E3	is the same as 1000
1.E3	is also 1000
1N3	is 1/1000, i.e. 0.001
3.7E6	is 3700000
-4.2N2	is -4.2/100, i.e. -0.042

(Note that neither Radio Shack Color LOGO nor TI LOGO accept
or handle numbers with decimal parts. They only accept integers.)
The 'E', for 'exponent', indicates that the number before it is to
be multiplied by 10 to the power given by the positive integer

after the digit. The 'N', for 'negative exponent', indicates that the number before it is to be divided by the appropriate power of 10 instead. In either case the power of ten to use is easily written and thought of as a '1' followed by the given number of '0's. There must be no spaces inside the number, and the integer which follows the 'E' or 'N' must be positive.

2.6.2 Other Arithmetic Procedures

Mainly for the sake of completeness, here are the other arithmetic procedures in Terrapin LOGO. If your LOGO system does not have them don't despair – you will (eventually) find that it is almost certainly possible to create them for yourself.

There are three trigonometric procedures. COS and SIN take one number as input – an angle in degrees – and output the cosine or sine of that angle:

    PRINT SIN 30

prints 0.5. The procedure ATAN takes two inputs, and outputs the angle in degrees whose arctangent is the second input divided by the first – try making the first input 0. The angle is always between 0 and 360.

There are various procedures which are concerned with integers (whole numbers) in particular, in one way or another. They are

INTEGER   This procedure takes one input and outputs the integer part of it, that is, it gets rid of any fractional part.

ROUND   This takes one input and outputs the nearest integer to it:

        PRINT ROUND 2.6   prints 3

        PRINT ROUND 2.47   prints 2

        PRINT ROUND −2.6   prints −3

REMAINDER This takes two inputs. If they are not integers it ROUNDs them first; it then outputs the remainder left when the first input is divided by the second:

        PRINT REMAINDER 75 11   prints 9

QUOTIENT This also takes two inputs, ROUNDing them first if necessary. It outputs the integer quotient of the first divided by the second:

   PRINT QUOTIENT 75 11   prints 6

  There are two other procedures, which are not especially concerned with integers:

SQRT This takes one input and outputs its square root. The input must of course be positive.

RANDOMIZE This takes no input and does not output anything. Its effect is to make the values produced by RANDOM even less predictable than they are. If you do not use RANDOMIZE, then whenever you start up LOGO and use RANDOM you will get the same sequence of random numbers.

2.7 MORE ABOUT DRAWINGS

All this knowledge can be put to use for constructing more elaborate and interesting drawings. However, there is one further LOGO topic that is worth knowing about first.

2.7.1 Controlling How The Screen Is Used

On the Apple II, part of a large drawing can be invisible, 'behind' the four lines of text at the bottom of the screen as in figure 2.6. Fortunately this is only one of the ways of utilising the screen permitted by the Apple II's electronics. The table below shows the choices, together with the corresponding Terrapin LOGO commands that select them. On other machines, with other LOGO systems, the possibilities and commands will be different and you should read your manual to find out more. The command DRAW, mentioned in section 1, automatically selects SPLITSCREEN. DRAW also clears the screen and returns the turtle to its initial position and heading. If you forget to use DRAW, your first drawing command will also cause a DRAW to happen. NODRAW also erases any drawing. When you are doing drawing, these control-key functions are extremely useful:

CTRL-F This has the effect of FULLSCREEN

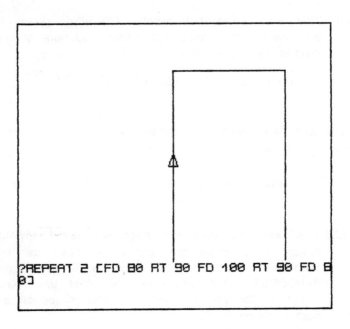

Figure 2.6

USING THE APPLE II SCREEN

SPLITSCREEN   Visible area: 280 wide
                                   200 high
                   Text area: bottom 4 lines

FULLSCREEN   Visible area: 280 wide
                                   240 high
                   Text area: none

NODRAW   No drawing at all
                   Text area: full 24 lines

CTRL-S This has the effect of SPLITSCREEN

CTRL-T ('T' for 'text') This makes the drawing invisible and makes
       the full 24 lines of text visible. It is not quite like
       NODRAW, because the drawing is not erased. You can
       make the drawing visible again by using CTRL-F or
       CTRL-S, but DRAW would erase the drawing.

The electronics also determine how colours look on the screen. As the correspondence between colours and turtle pen numbers are hard to remember and depend on your TV or monitor, it is a good idea to create some appropriately named variables, for example

```
MAKE "BLACK 0
MAKE "WHITE 1
MAKE "RED 2
MAKE "YELLOW 3
MAKE "BLUE 4
MAKE "GREEN 5
MAKE "INVERSE 6
```

These can be used with the PENCOLOR and BACKGROUND commands:

```
PC :RED
BG :WHITE
```

2.7.2 Putting Variables And Arithmetic To Use

If you have had some fancy graphics ideas in mind already, you may now be equipped to tackle them. Try them. If you find them still impossible, read on – there are yet more drawing commands to come. If you do not have a pet project, don't worry – there is no reason why you should, and there are many ways to get inspiration. One is to think about what what you have recently learnt about LOGO, and consider whether you can apply it to make interesting variations on what you had done previously. To make the most of this,

KEEP NOTES OF SUCCESSES

KEEP NOTES OF FAILURES – and what went wrong

KEEP NOTES OF IDEAS – especially half-baked ones

so that you can look back at them later. It is good practice to keep a notebook, or at least a supply of paper, close at hand for this. (Note for teachers: it is VERY IMPORTANT to get your pupils to do this. Do not be influenced by articles in the press suggesting that using a computer is a big step towards getting rid of paper.)

Here are two examples of the approach.

Spirals

In section 2.4 it was hinted that one way out of the sterile regularity which comes from overworking REPEAT is to vary some lengths from one repetition to the next. Variables are the way to do this. Figure 2.7 was produced by

```
MAKE "X 0
REPEAT 100 [FD :X RT 121 MAKE "X :X + 3]
```

The angle of 121 degrees is close to, but not equal to, the angle of 120 degrees used in drawing an equilateral triangle. Try some others:

44 or 46	(close to an octagon)
89 or 91	(close to a square)
71 or 73	(close to a pentagon)
143 or 145	(close to a pentagram)

but remember to MAKE "X 0 or some small number first, and to

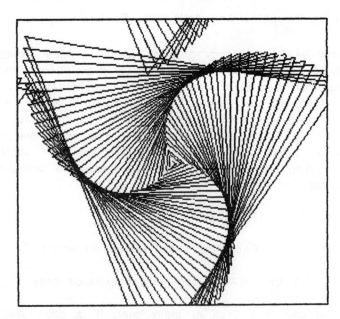

Figure 2.7

centre the turtle and clear the screen with

HOME CS

(Note for maths teachers: this exercise could be used to motivate the idea of experimenting with small changes in familiar situations.) There is nothing special about the number of repetitions – 100 seems a reasonable number. If it is too small the spiralling effect is not very clear. If it is too big the drawing overflows the screen, and if the turtle is being allowed to wrap the outcome can be very messy. It can be beautiful too, so try some examples nevertheless.

There are endless variations on spiralling. In the example above the length the turtle moves increases by 3 at each step while the angle it turns remains constant. What happens if it is the angle that increases, while the length stays constant? For instance,

```
MAKE "ANGLE 0
REPEAT 1000 [FD 3 RT :ANGLE
    MAKE "ANGLE :ANGLE + 7]
```

draws figure 2.8. The number of repetitions does need to be large here. Notice that there are 8 blobs, and the angle is increased by 7 degrees at each step. If the angle is increased by 11 degrees instead there are 12 blobs. With an increment of 13, there are 14 blobs. This suggests a simple rule relating the increment to the number of blobs. However, it is **not**

blobs = increment + 1

but something a bit more complex.

___

EXERCISES

(11)   What is the rule?

(12)   Investigate what happens when both the length and the angle vary. Try decrementing as well as incrementing.

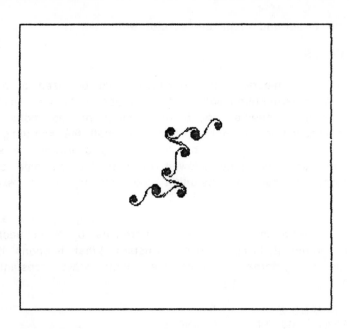

Figure 2.8

Random figures

To draw a rectangle of some random size it is not enough to

    REPEAT 4 [FD RANDOM 50 RT 90]

because each side in the drawing would be of random length, whereas rectangles have two pairs of equal sides. These commands do the trick:

    MAKE "W RANDOM 50
    MAKE "H RANDOM 50
    REPEAT 2 [FD :W RT 90 FD :H RT 90]

Therefore the following monster command will produce a sort of "instant Mondrian" picture[1]:

    REPEAT 100 [MAKE "W RANDOM 50 MAKE "H
        RANDOM 50 REPEAT 2 [FD :W RT 90 FD
        :H RT 90] FD RANDOM 100 RT 90 FD
        RANDOM 100 LT 90]

---

1 This isn't fair to Piet Mondrian, whose paintings are anything but random.

The anatomy of this is:

REPEAT 100 [(set up W) (set up H)
            (rectangle W units by H units)
            (move the turtle somewhere else)]

Figure 2.9 was drawn this way, with the turtle allowed to wrap. The final four commands (FD, RT, FD, LT) in the repetition are included to move the turtle away from the first corner of the rectangle it has just drawn. A PU and a PD command inserted on either side of these four commands would ensure that only complete rectangles appear in the drawing. However, after a hundred repetitions it should be almost impossible to see the extra lines where the turtle moved from one rectangle to the next.

As an example of making constructive use of unsuccessful ideas, look again at the first attempt to draw a single random rectangle. It did not draw one, and it was not state-transparent. The "instant Mondrian" command had to include some means of making sure that the repeated commands were not state-transparent. Repeating the 'unsuccessful' command might be an

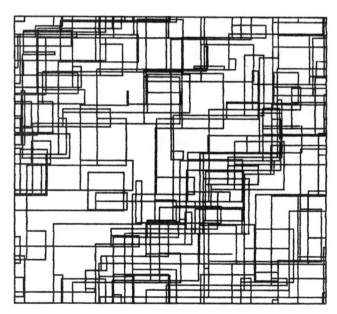

Figure 2.9

easy way to achieve similar results:

    REPEAT 25 [REPEAT 4 [FD RANDOM 50
        RT 90]]

This is the same as

    REPEAT 100 [FD RANDOM 50 RT 90]

a sample of which is shown in figure 2.10. (Note for teachers: this works because the intersection of two rectangles is a rectangle. It also works for triangles provided they are all of the same shape. It does not apply in quite the same way to pentagons, hexagons etc.)

There is nothing special about 100 as the number of repetitions. There is also nothing particularly vital about 90 as the turning angle in such a random figure. If the angle is made random and the length fixed the resulting drawing (such as figure 2.11) is a kind of random walk: Figure 2.11 was drawn by the following command. Try this with a much larger input to FORWARD

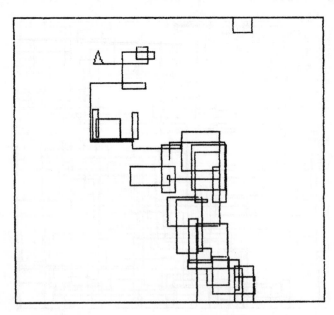

Figure 2.10

Figure 2.11

as well.

    REPEAT 1000 [FD 3 RT RANDOM 360]

EXERCISES

There are some interesting questions about random walks:

(13)   In a two-dimensional random walk, does the turtle tend to
        return to the starting point? Use NOWRAP to prevent wrap-
        ping, as that could cause confusion about whether the tur-
        tle had really returned to its start.

(14)   If so, roughly how many steps does it take? If not, does
        varying the range of angles make a difference, for exam-
        ple using RANDOM 90 or 90 * (RANDOM 4) instead?

(15)   Investigate one dimensional random walks, by using the
        expression 180 * (RANDOM 2) for the angle.

2.7.3 Cartesian Drawing Procedures

Most LOGO systems include procedures which control the turtle in a Cartesian way, that is, according to an (X,Y) co-ordinate system. In Terrapin LOGO the origin of co-ordinates is at the centre of the screen, so that the turtle's position co-ordinates can lie (give or take a small amount) in the ranges

$$-140 \leqslant X \leqslant 140 \qquad -120 \leqslant Y \leqslant 120$$

It is possible to change either of the turtle's co-ordinates, or both at once. The effect of doing any of these is to make the turtle leap to a new position on the screen. If the turtle's pen is down it will draw a straight line between the old position and the new one. The commands are

SETX   This takes one number, the turtle's new X co-ordinate, as input. If the pen is down a horizontal line will be drawn.

SETY   This takes one number, the turtle's new Y co-ordinate, as input. If the pen is down a vertical line will be drawn.

SETXY   This takes two numbers as inputs. The first is a new X co-ordinate, the second a new Y co-ordinate.

SETHEADING (or SETH for short).   This takes one number, the turtle's new heading, as input. It turns the turtle on the spot to point along that heading.

The following command should help you to get the feel of it:

    REPEAT 50 [SETXY (RANDOM 140) (RANDOM
        120)]

The parentheses are included only for clarity. The command draws a cat's cradle of lines, but only in the top right quarter of the screen where both co-ordinates are positive.   To cover the whole screen a random X co-ordinate between -140 and 140 is needed, and also a suitable Y co-ordinate. One possible way to do this is

    REPEAT 50 [SETXY (140 - RANDOM 280) (120
        - RANDOM 240)]

The Cartesian commands also provide a simple means of checking on the randomness of RANDOM. The idea is to use RANDOM to scatter small blips onto the screen; if it is done at random they should be evenly spread rather than clustered in places. The command FD 1 BK 1 draws a small blip, so

```
REPEAT 500 [PU SETXY (140 - RANDOM 280)
            (120 - RANDOM 240) PD FD 1 BK 1]
```

draws 500 blips at random places on the screen. It takes a while.

The SET- commands by themselves are not very convenient to use. They deal with absolute rather than relative positions on the screen and working in terms of absolute positions needs forethought. There is a complementary set of procedures whcih help to make the SET- ones much more useful. They are

XCOR   This takes no input, but outputs the turtle's current X co-ordinate. The command SETX XCOR thus does nothing at all. Note that the turtle's X co-ordinate cannot lie outside the range -140 to 140, even if the turtle has wrapped round an edge of the screen. If the turtle is at the right-hand side of the screen and it wraps round to the left-hand side, the X co-ordinate does not change smoothly as you do it. It jumps from around 140 to around -140.

YCOR   This takes no input, but outputs the turtle's current Y co-ordinate. It behaves much like XCOR.

HEADING This takes no input, but outputs the turtle's current heading. The heading is measured in degrees, in the range 0 to 360. A heading of 0 is directly up the screen, and the heading increases clockwise.

TOWARDS This takes two numbers as inputs, which it treats as the X and Y co-ordinates of a point on the screen. It outputs the heading that the turtle must have to aim at that point from its current location.

This set of procedures frees you from having to work in terms of absolute positions. The command

```
SETXY XCOR + 10 YCOR + 10
```

moves the turtle - drawing, if the pen is down - in a straight

line to a point 10 units right and 10 units up. It does not change
the heading. The command

    SETX XCOR + 2 SETX XCOR −2

makes the turtle draw a small horizontal blip in a state-
transparent way. It is also possible to record a position on the
screen for later use. for instance

    MAKE "X XCOR
    MAKE "Y YCOR
    MAKE "H HEADING
    SETXY :X :Y
    SETH :H

This is a very useful trick when constructing a drawing whcih
requires many commands. such as figure 2.12. It was drawn using
only Cartesian commands. Even simple drawings like this demand
quite a lot of typing. You would naturally hesitate to repeat this
effort every time you wanted to include a church or a house or
whatever in a drawing. There is a means of encapsulating a

Figure 2.12

sequence of commands as one (new) procedure, which can then be used in exactly the same way as existing procedures. Computer programming, after all, is supposed to help you avoid undue work rather than create it. Chapter 3 is about defining new procedures.

2.7.4 Curves

All the diagrams in this chapter have been composed of straight lines. There are no built-in Terrapin LOGO procedures immediately available to you for curve drawing (there are in some other LOGO versions). The material in chapter 3 will explain how to define some; this section is about the ideas involved.

Figure 2.8 suggests how curves can be simulated. The trick is approximation. Consider circles or arcs of circles, for example. The command

    REPEAT 360 [FD 1 RT 1]

draws a 360-sided polygon (very slowly)[1]. It is also as good a representation of a circle as the Apple II is going to allow. How big is this circle? Well, the circumference is 360 units so the radius must be 360 divided by 2π, or roughly 57.296. In general the circumference of a circle of radius R is $2\pi R$. To approximate to such a circle, therefore, the turtle must move FORWARD by $2\pi R/360$ for each step, and turn by 1 degree. Now $2\pi/360$ = 0.01745.., so a circle of a particular radius can be drawn by

    MAKE "R (radius)
    REPEAT 360 [FD :R*0.01745 RT 1]

(note that neither Radio Shack Color LOGO nor TI LOGO accept numbers with decimals, they only accept integers. You'll need to experiment.) To draw an arc of a circle just reduce the number of repetitions. To draw a rightward-bending arc which subtends a particular angle at the circle's centre,

    REPEAT (angle) [FD (radius)*0.01745 RT 1]

By looking at the command itself rather than what it drew, it

---

1 Except in Radio Shack Color LOGO, where it draws an octagon. The reason is that this LOGO has rather coarser ideas about the turtle's heading. Over a distance of 1 unit, it is not going to distinguish between a heading of 1 degree and a heading of 10 degrees. The cure is to make the step size and the angle increment bigger, perhaps around 8. That way you will get a reasonably circular-looking shape.

should be easy to see that the turtle will change its heading by the chosen angle in drawing the arc. A leftward-bending arc can be drawn by substituting LT for RT.

The drawing of a circle can be speeded up a bit, by commanding LOGO not to bother showing the turtle. The command is

HIDETURTLE (or HT for short)

and the complementary command is

SHOWTURTLE (or ST for short)

It is possible to approximate to curves other than circles, but it is usually much harder. Spirals probably represent the next step up in complexity – just make the radius increase slowly at each repetition. For instance,

```
MAKE "R 50
REPEAT 720 [FD :R*0.01745 RT 1 MAKE "R
    :R + 1]
```

draws two turns of a linear spiral. There is considerable scope for experimentation. Try changing the distance the turtle moves at each repetition as well, although stop it before this gets too big or it will become obvious that the curve is really made up of straight line segments. Another thing to do is to change the length or angle by multiplying by a constant less than 1 at each step, instead of adding a constant.

Chapter 3
Procedures

"Well," said Owl, "the customary procedure in
  such cases is as follows."
"What does Crustimony Proseedcake mean?" said
  Pooh. "For I am a Bear of Very Little Brain,
  and long words Bother me."
"It means the Thing to Do."

(Winnie-the-Pooh, A.A.Milne)

Aims Defining your own procedures offers an enormous range of
possibilities. This chapter explains how to create and modify
them. Doing so offers a great deal of power for experimenting with ideas. Later in the chapter, some advice and general principles are described that should help you to make
the most of this.

3.1 CREATING NEW PROCEDURES

IMPORTANT NOTE

Before starting work on this chapter, read the technical manual
that came with the LOGO system to find out how to prepare a
floppy disk (if your system uses them; cassettes might also need
preparing) so that it can be used for storing things in LOGO that
you want to keep. You need to do this **NOW** because you cannot
prepare one while running LOGO.

Suppose you wanted to draw a scene such as the one
shown in figure 3.1[1]. Drawing each house, tree and bird using

---

1 Maybe it is not something you would want to do, but just suppose for the sake of
argument...

only the basic turtle graphics commands would be extremely tedious. It would be easier if there were commands HOUSE, TREE and BIRD: the only difficulty might then be ensuring that the turtle was in the right place at the right time for each of these commands.

The ability to define such new commands, in terms of other commands, is an essential part of every version of LOGO. In Terrapin LOGO the procedures TO and EDIT let you do this. The same commands, with minor variations of detail, are used in most other versions of LOGO though Research Machines LOGO uses BUILD and CHANGE instead.

To see how to use TO, consider the following example. It is often convenient to have a command that will draw a box of some kind. Suppose the command is to be called BOX. The LOGO command

TO BOX

will erase any drawing and any text on the screen and instead

Figure 3.1

you should see essentially what is shown in figure 3.2. The line at the top is the **title line** of the new procedure BOX. The cursor is just under the 'T' of TO, and LOGO is now waiting for you to specify the sequence of commands that will make up the definition of BOX. You can now type commands, but LOGO will not obey them yet, even when you press RETURN – the cursor merely moves to the start of the next line. This is because you are now using a piece of the LOGO system called the **editor**. It helps to think of the editor as a tool for writing out the definition of a command which, when you finish editing, becomes known to the LOGO system. Try typing

```
REPEAT 4 [FD 50 RT 90]
END
```

and then pressing CTRL-C (that is, press the CTRL key and while holding it down press C). The screen should clear and the two messages

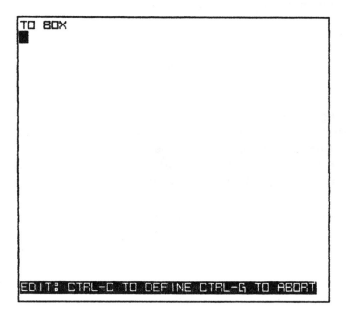

Figure 3.2

PLEASE WAIT...
BOX DEFINED

should appear, with a short pause before the second one, followed by the normal prompt. You can now use BOX as a normal command. Type

BOX

and press RETURN, and the turtle will draw a square of side 50. If it did something else instead then you may have made some mistake in typing the definition – read on...

When you use the editor you will find in at least three cases out of four that you want to change something or correct some typing mistake in an earlier line. Whatever the version of LOGO you are using, there are ways of moving the cursor around the screen, deleting parts of what you have typed and inserting new material. If you have already finished the editing of the definition you can get it back to modify it by the command

EDIT BOX

Terrapin LOGO gives you the following powers when using TO or EDIT:

- A single LOGO command line can, as before, stretch over several lines of the screen. However, when this happens (i.e. you type off the end of a line and onto the next line) the editor puts an exclamation mark at the right-hand side of the screen as a reminder that the line continues.

- The **arrow keys** move the cursor left or right. If the cursor is at the start of a line and is moved left, it jumps to the end of the line above. If the cursor is at the end of a line and is moved right it jumps to the start of the next line.

- Typing bits of LOGO inserts them at the point where the cursor is. If there is anything to the right of the cursor, that gets pushed to the right as you type.

- The **ESC** key, as before, can be used to delete a character (anything to the right of it on the same LOGO line – even if it spans more than one screen line – moves one place left to fill the gap). If the cursor is at the start of a line then the effect of the ESC key is to join that whole LOGO line onto the previous one.

There are also various CTRL-key options:

CTRL-P This moves the cursor **up** one LOGO line (the 'P' is for 'previous').

CTRL-N This moves the cursor **down** one LOGO line (the 'N' is for 'next').

CTRL-O This **opens** up a line – that is, it splices in a blank line where the cursor is.

CTRL-A This moves the cursor to the beginning of the LOGO line (think of 'A' being at the beginning of the alphabet).

CTRL-E This moves the cursor to the end of the line ('E' for 'end').

CTRL-K This deletes everything on the current LOGO line that is to the right of the cursor (the 'K' is for 'kill'). If there is nothing to the right of the cursor, it joins the current line to the next one.

The definition of a procedure may not fit into one screenful. This does not matter – just keep typing. The following CTRL-key functions should be useful in such a situation:

CTRL-B This moves you back by roughly a whole screenful in the definition (if possible), so that you can work on an earlier screenful.

CTRL-F This moves you forward by roughly a whole screenful (if possible) so that you can work on a later screenful.

CTRL-L This adjusts the definition so that the line with the cursor on it is in the centre of the screen.

As was mentioned earlier, CTRL-C is the way to end editing if you are satisfied with the definition. If you are not satisfied and want instead to abandon editing and discard the definition, type CTRL-G. This feature makes it easy to practise using the editor: just type

TO JUNK

or whatever, to get 'into' the editor and then try typing anything at all – a limerick, your name and address, rows of numbers. You can play around with the editing keys to your heart's content and eventually throw away all the messy results by typing CTRL-G – only do not type CTRL-C first! It is a **very** good idea to spend a little while doing this practice; everyone develops their own style of working with an editor and it is better to get a feel for it before using it in earnest.

Therefore, PRACTISE NOW.

(Notes for teachers: (a) get pupils to do this as an abstract exercise before they move on to defining procedures. It can be hard to think about editing and about the LOGO commands making up a definition at the same time (b) be careful about how you introduce LOGO procedures. Many beginners have trouble grasping the distinction between **defining** and **running** a procedure. They often expect the commands typed in as part of a definition to be obeyed at once – after all, they may never have articulated the notion of 'postponed action' to themselves before in any subject, and not just computer programming (c) if you have read the instructions above you may have noticed that the description of how to use the editor is based on a particular image, although it is not made explicit. The image is that of typing on a roll of paper seen through a window. The roll can be wound on (downward) by CTRL-F, and back (upward) by CTRL-B. Strips of blank paper can be spliced in by CTRL-O. It helps beginners to have some such analogy, though it is best not to press it too far if the reality cannot sustain it. Joining two lines into one using ESC is something that does not fit the analogy well, which is why the analogy is not explicitly stated above. It might still be worthwhile to use it if you are careful about the order in which the editing functions are introduced.)

3.2 PROCEDURES WITH INPUTS

The procedure BOX defined above can be put to use as though it were a normal LOGO command, e.g.

    REPEAT 36 [RT 10 BOX]

After a short while BOX will seem fairly limited. It would be better if it took an input which gave the size of the BOX. Procedures such as FORWARD and RIGHT take an input, so why not BOX? It can, once the definition is suitably changed. To do this, give the command

    EDIT BOX

and the definition of BOX will reappear. Remember that any drawing and any commands which were visible before the EDIT command will be erased by this. Use the editing functions to change the definition to look like this:

```
TO BOX :SIDE
REPEAT 4 [FD :SIDE RT 90]
END
```

The first line, called the **title line** has been changed by the addition of ':SIDE'. This informs the LOGO system, when you finish the editing, that BOX will in future take one input which, **for the purposes of the definition**, will be a variable called by the name SIDE. This variable only exists while BOX **is being run,** and it **temporarily** supersedes any previously existing variable called SIDE. Therefore the last of the commands

```
MAKE "SIDE 100
BOX 50
PRINT :SIDE
```

will print 100, because the command BOX has finished by the time the PRINT command is given.

A procedure can have as many inputs as you like. The names of the inputs can also be given at the time you invoke the editor, for example

```
TO TRASH :N1 :RHUBARB :DISTANCE
```

and then that will be what is shown at the top of the screen. Once into the editor, you are free to change the title line as you like, provided that there is a valid title line when you finish the editing.

To reinforce the point about inputs, look at these two procedures:

```
TO JUNK1 :N
JUNK2
END
```

```
TO JUNK2
PRINT :N
END
```

(it is legal and commonplace to define two or more procedures in one piece of editing. That is the only real significance of END, to mark where one definition ends where and another should start). With these,

```
MAKE "N 100
JUNK1 50
```

will result in the number 50 being printed. Although it is JUNK2 that is responsible for a number being printed, JUNK1 is still running when JUNK2 gets obeyed (because the command JUNK2 is part of the definition of JUNK1), so the variable called N whose value is printed is really the input to JUNK1.

Digression:

> If it seems to you as though the form of the TO and EDIT commands contradicts the rules about naming and when to use a colon or a quote, you are correct. This is a peculiarity of Terrapin LOGO and one or two other versions.

A 'box' does not have to mean a square, it can mean anything polygonal. Here is BOX modified to take two inputs, the first of which is to be the side length and the second is to be the number of sides:

```
TO BOX :SIDE :N
REPEAT :N [FD :SIDE RT 360/:N]
END
```

Now the command

```
BOX 50
```

will result in an error message saying that there are not enough inputs for BOX. The command

```
BOX 50 6
```

will draw a hexagon, and

```
MAKE "N 3
REPEAT 18 [BOX :N 6 RT 10 MAKE "N :N+3]
```

will draw figure 3.3. The example used in this chapter so far, drawing a box, may not look like a particularly good advertisement for procedures as labour-saving devices. The next subsection should help to dispel doubts.

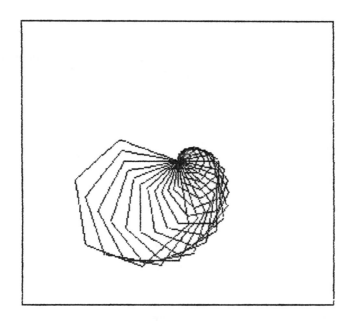

Figure 3.3

3.3 CRUDE ANIMATION - A STUDY

It is possible, in Terrapin LOGO, to achieve a crude form of animation. In some versions of LOGO it is not really possible, and in
others it is very much easier. The difference is mainly caused by
differences in computer hardware rather than software.

At this point, the value of LOGO as a tool for experimenting
starts to appear - for there are a variety of ways to set about
animating something. Suppose that the objective is to animate a
small square to make it appear to move around the screen. There
are at least two ways this might be done:

A   (a)   draw the box on the screen,

      (b)   move the turtle a little, with the pen up,

      (c)   clear the screen,

      (d)   repeat steps (a) to (c) many times.

or

B   (a)   draw the box on the screen,

     (b)   erase the box by redrawing it in the background colour, perhaps after a short pause,

     (c)   move the turtle a little, with the pen up,

     (d)   repeat steps (a) to (c) many times.

At first sight there is not much to choose between these as basic methods. It would be nice if the basic method could be extended, for instance

-   to allow acceleration or deceleration of the shape

-   to allow motion along curves

-   to allow size changes so that the shape appears to be getting nearer or further away.

The rest of this subsection will be devoted to showing one typical route for the investigation and development of one of these methods, namely method B. The question of whether method A has any relative advantages or disadvantages will be left as an exercise.

Assume that the background colour is 0, the pen is down and the pen colour is unknown. Then step (a) is

    PC 1 BOX 10 4

The initial PC (that's PENCOLOR, remember?) ensures that the turtle will draw the box, in colour 1. Step (b) is just

    PC 0 BOX 10 4

Forget about the business of a delay before erasing, for the moment at least. Step (c) is just

    PU FD 10 PD

This assumes that 'a little' means 10 units. Remember that PU is short for PENUP and PD is short for PENDOWN. All these can be combined in one procedure called ANIMATE:

    TO ANIMATE

```
PC 1 BOX 10 4
PC 0 BOX 10 4
PU FD 10 PD
END
```

Now tidy up the screen and then try it, by

```
HOME CS
REPEAT 50 [ANIMATE]
```

The result is remarkably disappointing. It is not at all fast, and the turtle leaping about all over the drawing spoils any impression of motion by the box itself. This does not mean that animation is impossible. In such a situation, there are two things you should do. The first is to remind yourself that in 90% of cases it will turn out that there is more to the problem than appears at first glance. The second is to analyse why the result is disappointing. Writing down what the snags are helps a lot; then, when other difficulties appear later on, your notes will help you to avoid fal-ling into the same old traps. In this case, perhaps the two diffi-culties – slowness and the mad dancing of the turtle – are related. It may be that the time spent by LOGO in drawing the turtle at the end of each FD and RT command is why it is so slow. The cure is to dispense with the turtle somehow. Is there a way of doing this? Yes, the command HT (short for HIDETURTLE) instructs the LOGO system not to bother showing the turtle. Try it:

```
HOME CS
HT REPEAT 50 [ANIMATE]
```

It is better, but still poor. There are two 'motions' visible – the turtle round the square in the BOX command, and the jerky motion of the square. The second might be made less jerky by reducing the turtle motion between one square and the next, by changing the FD 10 in the last line of ANIMATE to FD 5 or thereabouts. Doing this helps the situation a little, but also makes it clear that the motion of the turtle around the square in BOX is the main snag.

Getting round this looks impossible. There is no Terrapin LOGO command to make the turtle draw faster. One possibility is to make the box even smaller – say 5 units on a side – but it is rather weak-willed to have to accept that it is only possible to animate tiny shapes. Therefore the question comes down to this: is there any other way to draw a square, a way that does not use FD? Presumably BK is just as inadequate for the task as FD, although it is worth a try. The answer is yes, there are the Cartesian commands. You may have noticed that they are fast, though that is only an impression at this stage. However, how can BOX be modified to use Cartesian commands? Drawing a hexagon, for example, must be difficult because the co-ordinates will never be straightforward integers.

A useful principle to call on at this point is

If you cannot crack the problem, avoid it.

The command BOX is too general for this investigation. A command that draws a small square is all that is required. The way forward is to edit ANIMATE to replace the BOX commands by (say) SQUARE and to define SQUARE suitably using Cartesian commands. SQUARE can be defined in the same editing session as changing ANIMATE, by moving the cursor past the end of the definition of ANIMATE and typing in the definition of SQUARE, or it can be defined separately:

```
TO ANIMATE
PC 1 SQUARE
PC 0 SQUARE
PU FD 10 PD
END

TO SQUARE
SETX XCOR + 10
SETY YCOR + 10
SETX XCOR - 10
SETY YCOR - 10
END
```

Be careful: editing not only erases the drawing, it also undoes the effect of HT and returns the turtle to its default state of being shown on the screen after every drawing command. Each of the four lines in SQUARE draws one side of the square. The square it draws has its sides parallel to the sides of the screen whatever the heading of the turtle, but that is not a particular handicap. In fact, it could be an advantage; in the earlier version the motion of the square was always parallel to a side of the square. If you try this version of ANIMATE you should find that it is much better. In Terrapin LOGO the Cartesian commands are significantly faster than FD and BK, even with the turtle hidden.

At last the basic idea, method B, looks workable. Having established this, it is time to think about embellishments. Look once more at the definition of ANIMATE. Having cut out the use of FD in drawing the square, it might well be advantageous to cut out the use of FD there too. Replacing it by a SETX command is too restrictive, but a SETXY command should do. The amount by which to change the X and Y co-ordinates could be inputs to ANIMATE:

```
TO ANIMATE :X :Y
PC 1 SQUARE
PC 0 SQUARE
PU SETXY XCOR + :X YCOR + :Y PD
END
```

Try various values for the inputs. Beware of this, however:

```
HOME CS
HT REPEAT 50 [ANIMATE 10 -10]
```

Terrapin LOGO will tell you that ANIMATE needs more inputs, because it takes the ANIMATE command to be ANIMATE (10-10) rather than ANIMATE 10 (-10). The way to avoid this trap is to use parentheses to make the meaning clear.

ANIMATE can be further improved. At present it does only one movement of the square. Suppose that a final line is added:

```
TO ANIMATE :X :Y
PC 1 SQUARE
PC 0 SQUARE
PU SETXY XCOR + :X YCOR + :Y PD
ANIMATE :X :Y
END
```

This is legal because, at the time ANIMATE is run, the LOGO system knows how to obey the ANIMATE command in the last line! This idea of a procedure invoking itself, whether in the last line or elsewhere, is called **recursion.** It is a very powerful technique, and it will be used a lot later in this book. The new version of ANIMATE does one movement of the square, then invokes ANIMATE. So, what it does is to move the square once, then ... move the square once, then ... move the square once, then ... etc. Before you try it you had better make sure that you know how to stop it. In Terrapin LOGO, the way is to type CTRL-G. This **always stops whatever is happening and gets you back to the prompt.** (Note for teachers: 'G' for 'give up'? Whichever mnemonic you choose, use it. There is no virtue in trying to use computer jargon such as 'CTRL-G causes an execution interrupt'.) With recursion, all that is needed to start the animation is

```
HOME CS
ANIMATE 10 2
```

for example. The REPEAT command is unnecessary. If it is used, only the first repetition will happen. Typing CTRL-G will stop everything, including the REPEAT.

Another embellishment is the 'zoom lines' effect common in early Walt Disney cartoons. An easy way to achieve it is to have several (say three) squares always visible. Whenever one is added to the screen, the idea is not to delete it but to delete the fourth square back instead. Here is one way to do this:

```
TO ANIMATE :X :Y
PC 1 SQUARE
PU SETXY XCOR - 3*:X YCOR - 3*:Y PD
PC 0 SQUARE
PU SETXY XCOR + 4*:X YCOR + 4*:Y PD
END
```

The first SETXY in this leaps the turtle from the latest square, back past the previous two to the starting position of the third last square. That square is deleted. The second SETXY leaps the turtle past the newly added square to the starting position for the next ANIMATE. The whole effect is much more pleasing, even if very crude as an example of computer animation. (Note: one curiosity of the Apple II's electronics is that you are likely to get odd fragments of colour appearing on the screen, depending on the inputs to ANIMATE! If you have used colour graphics on the Apple II before you will be used to this.)

EXERCISES

(1)   How can acceleration and/or deceleration of the square be simulated?

(2)   Is it practicable to make the square grow or shrink as it moves? Can motion toward or away from you be simulated by this?

(3)   Is it practicable to make the square change orientation as it moves? (It might help you to remember that LOGO provides procedures for SIN and COS).

(4)   Does moving along a non-linear path spoil the animation effect? One way to start on this would be to consider changing the inputs to the recursive ANIMATE command within the definition of ANIMATE, by a small fixed amount each time it invokes itself.

(5)   What are the relative merits of using basic method A for animation instead?

3.4 THOUGHTS ABOUT WORKING WITH PROCEDURES

Look again at figure 3.1 on page 50, which showed some houses, trees and birds. There are various ways to set about the task of making such a drawing. Each way has its pros and cons. The next two subsections will consider fundamentally different approaches.

3.4.1 A Bottom Up Approach

One way to start is to get a sheet of graph paper and plot roughly where everything is to go. Going to the lengths of actually drawing the whole scene on paper is too much like real work; the point is to make sure that none of the houses and none of the birds overlap any other. To do this it is necessary to decide on the size of a house and on the size of a bird (are different sizes of bird to be allowed?). Thereafter you can start on defining the procedures which will be used for a house. A house in this scene will have a body (the main rectangular part), a roof, a door and a window. Suppose the body is to be 20 units across and 10 units high. The door ought to be near one side (the left, say) and perhaps 4 wide and 7 high. The window will be perhaps 5 square. Assume that the turtle is to start at the lower left corner of the body and with a heading of 0 degrees. Some playing might get you to this definition, or something similar:

```
TO HOUSE
REPEAT 2 [FD 10 RT 90 FD 20 RT 90]
RT 90 FD 4 LT 90
REPEAT 2 [FD 7 RT 90 FD 4 RT 90]
LT 90 FD 4 RT 90
RT 90 FD 12 LT 90 PU FD 3 PD
REPEAT 4 [FD 5 RT 90]
PU BK 3 PD LT 90 FD 12 RT 90
FD 10 RT 45 FD 5.66
RT 45 FD 12 RT 45 FD 5.66 RT 135
FD 20 RT 90 BK 10
END
```

This is almost incomprehensible. It is easier to break it up into suitable chunks, like this:

```
TO BODY
REPEAT 2 [FD 10 RT 90 FD 20 RT 90]
END

TO DOOR
RT 90 FD 4 LT 90
REPEAT 2 [FD 7 RT 90 FD 4 RT 90]
LT 90 FD 4 RT 90
END

TO WINDOW
RT 90 FD 12 LT 90 PU FD 3 PD
REPEAT 4 [FD 5 RT 90]
PU BK 3 PD LT 90 FD 12 RT 90
END

TO ROOF
FD 10 RT 45 FD 5.66
RT 45 FD 12 RT 45 FD 5.66 RT 135
FD 20 RT 90 BK 10
END

TO HOUSE
BODY DOOR WINDOW ROOF
END
```

This is slightly easier, although exactly the same basic commands are used and in the same order. Each of the procedures assumes the same starting place for the turtle, and requires some care to define considering the simplicity of the resulting drawing of a house. Are you convinced that the definitions are correct? Did you check them or did you sensibly baulk at that mundane task? On the other hand there is this to be said, each of the ingredients is state-transparent and so the definition of HOUSE in terms of BODY, DOOR, WINDOW and ROOF is child's play. This sort of approach, where the ingredients are tackled separately and almost in isolation, and are combined only at the last stage, is widely known as **bottom up**. Progress of the work is from the **bottom** (or specific) level up towards the **top** (or general) level.

3.4.2 A Top Down Approach

Instead of diving straight into the fine detail you could start with generalities. For example, a house in this scene consists of a body, a door, a roof and a window and so the definition of HOUSE can be

```
TO HOUSE
BODY DOOR ROOF WINDOW
```

END

and it remains to define these four ingredients. The body, door and window are all rectangles even though the window is a special case, viz. a square. Thus BODY can be defined as

```
TO BODY
RECTANGLE 10 20
END
```

provided that RECTANGLE's first input is going to be its height and its second is going to be the width. In HOUSE, the BODY is followed by the DOOR. This could be expressed as

```
TO DOOR
MOVE.FROM.BODY.TO.DOOR
RECTANGLE 7 4
END
```

where MOVE.FROM.BODY.TO.DOOR does what its name suggests. Note that it is acceptable to have full stops within a name, and it makes a compound name more readable. Similarly,

```
TO WINDOW
MOVE.FROM.DOOR.TO.WINDOW
RECTANGLE 5 5
END
```

```
TO ROOF
MOVE.FROM.WINDOW.TO.ROOF
RT 45 FD 5.66 RT 45 FD 12 RT 45 FD 5.66
MOVE.FROM.ROOF.TO.BODY
END
```

There are still five undefined procedures, but assumptions have already been made about each of them. For instance, in MOVE.FROM.DOOR.TO.WINDOW the turtle starts from where it finished after DOOR, and must end at the starting place for drawing the rectangular outline of the window. (Note for pedants: all those MOVE.FROM.somewhere.TO.somewhere could indeed have been incorporated explicitly in the definition of HOUSE, for example

```
TO HOUSE
BODY MOVE.FROM.BODY.TO.DOOR
DOOR MOVE.FROM.DOOR.TO.WINDOW
WINDOW MOVE.FROM.WINDOW.TO.ROOF
ROOF MOVE.FROM.ROOF.TO.BODY
END
```

and that makes it slightly easier to remember the necessary

assumptions. But it requires more forethought at the start and it does not save any work. An exhaustive discussion would be exhausting.)

You can define the extra procedures for yourself. This sort of approach goes by the name of **top down**; progress is from the top (or general) level towards the bottom (or specific) level.

3.4.3 Comparing The Two Approaches

The 'bottom up' approach often leads to defining unduly elaborate procedures, such as those on page XX. Three of those four contain a LOGO command to draw some size of rectangle, and it would have been neater to define a general rectangle procedure to use in those three. Doing that is **not** much less work, but at least the rectangle procedure would thereafter exist as a general tool for other uses as well. For example, you could decide, in due course, that the house is really in need of a chimney. It would be much easier to experiment with its size if there were a general rectangle procedure available.

Another point against working 'bottom up' is that your procedures are harder to read and harder to extend later on. The decisions made while defining the procedures are not even hinted at by anything visible within them, they are only recorded elsewhere – on paper at best, more commonly solely in your head. On the other hand working 'bottom up' is 'natural' and easy to start with. When visualising a drawing, the semantically complete components such as 'door' and 'window' are what catches the attention rather than incomplete ingredients such as 'side of door' and 'top of roof'. But, when you start defining the sequence of LOGO commands, it is the details such as angles and lengths which are the focus of attention and this makes 'bottom up' working the 'natural' way.

Working 'top down' is much cleaner once you are used to it. Unfortunately it does take a while to get used to. However, because you begin by representing general chunks of the drawing by procedure names before defining the procedures themselves, it is natural to choose the names so as to remind you of the decisions, such as MOVE.FROM.BODY.TO.DOOR. When you return later to extend or change the drawing, it is easier to pick up the threads. It is also easier to do the actual modifications. Take an example: suppose that HOUSE is not the right size for some particular purpose. You resolve to give HOUSE an input which is a scale factor, so that HOUSE 1.5 is half as big again as HOUSE 1. In both the 'top down' and 'bottom up' cases the new HOUSE procedure might be

```
TO  HOUSE  :SCALE
BODY DOOR WINDOW ROOF
END
```

(Note that it is unnecessary to give BODY etc. an input, though it is up to you. The temporary variable SCALE will exist while they are being run, so the definition of these procedures can use it.) In the 'bottom up' versions of BODY etc., you need to append the LOGO phrase '* :SCALE' to every FD and BK command – a total of sixteen times. In the 'top down' case you need only do this twelve times – twice inside the definition of rectangle, three times inside ROOF, once in MOVE.FROM.BODY.TO.DOOR and twice each in the other MOVE... procedures.

Contrary to popular programming folklore, the 'top down' approach is **not** appreciably easier to work with, although it is easier to read and understand once the whole thing works. There is just as much scope for mis-remembering decisions made at an earlier stage of the enterprise, or perhaps even more. A very common occurrence is to forget to define some procedure at all first time round, although this is not hazardous but merely frustrating in LOGO. Getting used to 'top down' working calls for some effort, particularly in learning to plan and analyse first then act later. This does not mean that you have to map out the entire campaign beforehand; it merely means learning to remind yourself to take a second look at what you are visualising, and learning to generalise.

Very few people, even sampled from professional programmers, stick purely to one approach or the other. The vast majority use a hybrid of the two and the ease and flexibility of the solution depends on the particular mix. As a general principle, if one is needed,

top down is the one to choose if you are tackling something unknown or if you expect to want to generalise your work later on

bottom up is for when you are on familiar ground.

3.4.4 Afterthought

Adding the birds is the major hurdle on the way to finishing figure 3.1. Each is made of two arcs, and arcs were the topic in section 2.7.4 in chapter 2. It is worthwhile to define procedures for arcs; for instance

```
TO ARCRIGHT :RADIUS :ANGLE
REPEAT :ANGLE [FD :RADIUS * 0.01745
      RT 1]
END
```

Notice that the angle has to be positive (LOGO will object if it is negative) but the radius can be any number. An ARCLEFT procedure is useful even though ARCRIGHT with a negative radius will do the trick.

Drawing a bird by joining two arcs is still not entirely trivial – try it – but it is fairly easy to experiment with, once you have a tool such as ARCRIGHT at your command. You can reasonably expect to get it wrong two or three times before getting it right, so don't kick yourself the first time! The rules are

(a) make procedures which are tools, when you can, and

(b) in general, generalise.

3.5 ANOTHER STUDY – A TICKING CLOCK

The aim of this is to draw a clock face, and make it keep to time. There are three separate chunks clearly involved: drawing the clock face, drawing the hands and making the clock work. Figure 3.4 shows a simple clock face, drawn by

```
TO MARK
PU FD 50 PD FD 10 PU BK 60 PD
END

HOME CS
REPEAT 12 [MARK RT 30]
```

The procedure MARK is state-transparent, and it is assumed that the turtle starts and ends at the centre of the clock face. A better face might have the marks for 12, 3, 6 and 9 o'clock slightly longer than the rest. A further refinement would be to add Roman numerals – much easier to draw than arabic numerals – but it is best to start with something very simple.

The other two chunks are not so easy. It is tempting to launch into the task of drawing the hands and give no thought to the other one. Doing so will probably get you into a mess, because making the clock tick involves redrawing the hands once per minute. Consider that first, therefore. A command such as

```
REPEAT 1000 [TICK]
```

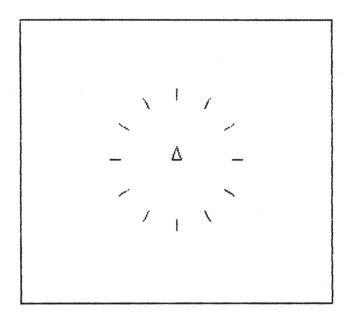

Figure 3.4

would be all that is needed, if TICK advances the hands by a minute and then takes a minute to finish. The clock will wind down after 1000 minutes, but if you seriously want to leave your computer switched on and doing nothing else for much longer than 16 hours you can simply increase the number of repetitions. Thus the problem is only how to define TICK. Look at the phrase 'advances the hands'. Where are they advanced from, and where to? This suggests having two variables, one concerned with the minute hand and one with the hour hand. Call them MINUTE and HOUR. The value of MINUTE will be the heading of the minute hand; it would have been equally reasonable to elect that the values should be the number of minutes since the clock was started. TICK must do this at least:

- erase the minute hand,

- erase the hour hand,

- update the MINUTE and HOUR variables,

- draw the minute hand in its new place,

-    draw the hour hand in its new place

The minute hand must not be long enough to reach the hour marks on the face or it will erase them as it moves; let it be 40 units long, and let the hour hand be 20 units long. Then the erasing of the minute hand can be done by

```
PC 0
SETH :MINUTE FD 40 BK 40
```

The hour hand is erased in the same way. The next task is updating MINUTE and HOUR. As there are 60 minutes in an hour, and 360 degrees to be swept by the minute hand, the command is

```
MAKE "MINUTE :MINUTE + 6
```

and, for the hour hand,

```
MAKE "HOUR :HOUR + 0.5
```

Here is a prototype for TICK:

```
TO TICK
PC 0
SETH :MINUTE FD 40 BK 40
SETH :HOUR FD 20 BK 20
MAKE "MINUTE :MINUTE + 6
MAKE "HOUR :HOUR + 0.5
PC 1
SETH :MINUTE FD 40 BK 40
SETH :HOUR FD 20 BK 20
END
```

Unfortunately it only takes moments rather than a full minute, when it is run. What is needed is a delaying command, something that does nothing but takes a while. Tests will show you that

```
REPEAT 61000 []
```

is such a command (even doing nothing takes a little time!), and that 61000 is approximately the right number if you add the command as the last line of TICK. You will need to adjust it slightly to make the clock accurate.

One oddity of TICK is that the first time it is used, it erases non-existent hands, but this does not matter. It only remains to put all the ingredients together. Remember to set the values of

MINUTE and HOUR before starting the clock.

EXERCISES

(6)   Is it practicable to include a second hand?

(7)   Define a procedure which takes two numbers as input,
        representing the time of day, and draws the clock and
        starts it.

(8)   Create a clock that runs backwards, or only has six hours
        on its face. Find out if other people can get used to
        using such a clock.

3.6 MORE ABOUT PROCEDURES

All the examples in this chapter so far have been concerned with
drawing. Some have used inputs, others have not. None have
output anything. It is reasonable to want to define procedures that
output, and LOGO, being a very reasonable language, provides a
means of doing so. In Terrapin LOGO there is a procedure OUT-
PUT, which takes one input. Its effect is to end the procedure in
which it appears, and make it output whatever OUTPUT's input
was. Here is an example:

```
TO SQUARE :N
OUTPUT :N * :N
END
```

The command

```
PRINT SQUARE 7
```

will print 49, because the OUTPUT procedure has input 49, and
causes SQUARE to end and output 49. Note that SQUARE does
not resume (so to speak) – if SQUARE were instead

```
TO SQUARE :N
OUTPUT :N * :N
PRINT "CLOWN
END
```

then PRINT SQUARE 7 would still only print 49, because obeying the OUTPUT is taken by LOGO to be a sign to stop obeying the definition of SQUARE.

Digression:

> Suppose that were not so? Then you could put two OUT-PUTs in a procedure definition, and LOGO would get very confusing. If you have ever fancied trying your hand at specifying a new programming language, this suggests an intriguing possibility on which to base something...

Another common factor of all the examples so far is that all the commands in a procedure definition are obeyed, none depend on any kind of circumstance. Being able to do one thing if some condition prevails and another thing if not, is what makes computers so useful. A facetious but comprehensible example, which nevertheless calls for a sophisticated computer system and a lot of programming work, is

> if....it is Friday
> and...it is near the end of the day,
> then..remind the users that the computer closes
> down at 6 p.m.

Note that there is an implied 'else..do not remind them' here. This example would require that the computer can find out the date and time, that it has a means (expressed in the form of a program) of judging what 'near the end of the day' means, and that it has a means of reminding users. Of course, nobody would be single-minded enough to do all the programming work needed to make this example possible, unless the work could also be put to many other such uses.

In LOGO, and in most programming languages, the kind of conditions which it is possible to make some action or command depend upon are very simple. What complicates the matter is that it is very handy to be able to compound conditions, such as 'this condition **and** that condition' or 'this **or** that'. Since these are themselves conditions it must also be possible to have conditions such as 'this condition **and** (that condition **or** another condition)' and so on.

In Terrapin LOGO conditional commands look like this:

IF :N > 0 THEN MAKE "Z :N

This says that 'if the value of N is greater than 0 then give Z the value of N'.

```
IF :N = 0 THEN PRINT "HELP ELSE
      MAKE "N :N - 1
```

This is 'if the value of N is 0 then print the word HELP, else make N one less than its present value'.

In general such commands must be of the form

IF condition THEN command(s)

or

IF condition THEN command(s) ELSE command(s)

although there is one further way of expressing the idea which will be mentioned shortly.

Digression for Apple LOGO users:
Apple LOGO is very like Terrapin LOGO, but is significantly different here. The Apple LOGO conditional commands are

IF condition [command(s) if true]

IF condition [command(s) if true] [command(s) if not]

and you will need to translate the examples in this book if you are using Apple LOGO. The translation is easy: turn 'THEN' into '[', put ']' at the very end of any IF command, and replace 'ELSE' by '] ['. For example,

IF :N = 0 THEN PRINT "ME ELSE PRINT "YOU

becomes

IF :N = 0 [PRINT "ME] [PRINT "YOU]

There are numerous possibilities for the condition in these commands. As the examples above suggest, it can be

something > anotherthing

something = anotherthing

something < anotherthing

where the 'somethings' and 'anotherthings' are numbers. In the case of 'something = anotherthing' they can also be words, or even another kind of object altogether called lists – these are introduced in chapter 4. In fact, in LOGO a condition is really just the word TRUE or the word FALSE or any expression that outputs TRUE or FALSE; each of the above conditions does that, so

    PRINT 3 > 4

prints FALSE, and

    PRINT 7 * 7 > 30

prints TRUE.

There are other possibilities for conditions. They can be any procedure which outputs the word TRUE or the word FALSE. For instance, suppose a number is to be deemed huge if it is bigger than 1000. The procedure

```
TO HUGE :NUMBER
IF :NUMBER > 1000 THEN OUTPUT "TRUE
    ELSE OUTPUT "FALSE
END
```

can be used as a condition:

    IF HUGE :X THEN PRINT "COLOSSAL!

Conditions can be compounded by using the procedures ALLOF and ANYOF. Each of these normally takes two inputs, which must be TRUE or FALSE, and outputs one of TRUE or FALSE, for example

    PRINT ALLOF 4 > 2 71 < 70

prints FALSE because not all are true.

However, it is sometimes necessary to check whether ALLOF or ANYOF a fair number of conditions are true. There is, accordingly, a convenient way of doing this in LOGO. The rule is that ALLOF and ANYOF can actually have any number of inputs provided that the whole collective condition is enclosed in parentheses, for example

```
IF ( ANYOF XCOR > 135 YCOR > 115
    XCOR < -135 YCOR < -115 ) THEN
    PRINT "OOPS!
```

If parentheses are not used then there must be exactly two inputs for ALLOF or ANYOF. The same kind of rule happens to apply to the procedure PRINT, and to a very few other procedures that will appear in chapter 4.

There are some procedures built into Terrapin LOGO for checking certain kinds of condition. The procedure NUMBER? takes one input, and outputs TRUE only if the input is a number (rather than, say, a word). The procedure WORD? outputs TRUE only if its input is a word. The procedure THING? expects a word as its input, and outputs TRUE only if there is a variable by that name[1]. The procedure NOT is very useful. Its input must be the word TRUE or the word FALSE – whichever it is, NOT outputs the other one.

EXERCISES

Suppose you have typed in the commands

```
MAKE "ALPHA 6
MAKE "BETA 9
MAKE "GAMMA -12
```

(9)   What does this do?

```
IF NOT :ALPHA < 10 THEN PRINT "RATS
```

(10)   What does this do?

```
IF ( ANYOF :ALPHA < 5 :BETA < 5
     :GAMMA < 5 ) THEN PRINT "OK
ELSE PRINT "HAGGIS
```

(11)   What does this do?

```
PRINT ALLOF :ALPHA > :BETA 0 > :GAMMA
```

(12)   What does this do?

```
PRINT :GAMMA / :ALPHA + :BETA = 7
```

(13)   What does this do?

```
IF THING "GAMMA THEN PRINT "EXISTS ELSE
```

---

1 In other LOGO books you will find this expressed another way, namely that THING? only outputs TRUE if the variable has a value. The notion implied by this is that every possible variable exists, but most have no value! (Note for teachers: beware of such a notion. There are an immense number of possible variables, and an Apple II is physically quite small .. so where are they?)

PRINT "NON-EXISTENT

3.6.1 An Example – Bouncing The Turtle

The aim of the experiment in this sub-section is to make the turtle appear to bounce back from the edges of the screen as it
moves around (see figure 3.5). One way to start is to figure out
how to make the turtle seem to move continuously. This need be
nothing more sophisticated than repeating the command FD 5 (the
number 5 being just a typical small number). What happens near
the edge? Clearly, the turtle's heading has to change, but by
what? Take a specimen case: the turtle is moving along a heading
of 73 degrees and comes to the right-hand side. A nice effect
would be if the turtle's heading changed to –73 degrees. Thinking about some more specimen cases suggest the following rules

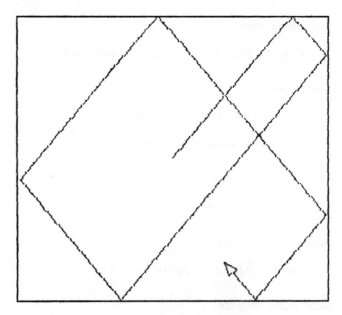

Figure 3.5

- if the turtle 'hits' either side its heading H should change to −H

- if the turtle 'hits' the top or bottom, its heading H should change to (180−H).

The remaining problem is how to find out when the turtle is nearing a side. The easy way is to check its co-ordinates. Rather than redirecting the turtle exactly when it hits the edge, do the simple thing and redirect it if it is close to the edge, for example if XCOR > 135. Testing whether the turtle is close to an edge ought to be done at every move, since any move might be the one which takes it near an edge. Here is a procedure STEP to make one 5 unit turtle step; the turtle motion will be done by repeating STEP:

```
TO STEP
IF ANYOF XCOR > 135 XCOR < -135 THEN
     SETH ( - HEADING )
IF ANYOF YCOR > 115 YCOR < -115 THEN
     SETH ( 180 - HEADING )
FD 5
END
```

Before trying this, think a minute. There seems to be a possibility not accounted for − what if the turtle comes to two edges simultaneously, when it approaches a corner of the screen? As it happens this is a red herring − the definition of STEP is adequate for this circumstance too (or is that wrong?).

Try STEP, but give the turtle an unusual heading first, for example

```
HOME CS
SETH 37
REPEAT 500 [STEP]
```

You can modify STEP by adding the command STEP to the end of the definition. Then the REPEAT command can be replaced by the command STEP alone, because it will repeat itself.

One of STEP's deficiencies is that the screen fills up with diagonal lines pretty swiftly and it becomes hard to see the bouncing effect. A cure is to change things so that the turtle appears to be towing a piece of string − as the turtle moves, the line 50 units back along its path must be erased. Since the task of figuring out where the turtle was some distance back along a path which might have corners in it looks hard, do it another way.

Instead. imagine that there are two turtles[1] moving independently, with one drawing and one erasing. Because there is only one tur- tle in Terrapin LOGO, it must leap about a lot to achieve this effect; the position and heading of each hypothetical turtle can be recorded by variables, and updated at each leap of the real turtle. You can work out the details for yourself. Do try it, because many of the mistakes you can make in this project give you different and very pleasing effects!

3.6.2 Another Sort Of Conditional Command

Terrapin LOGO has a useful alternative to IF .. THEN .. ELSE.. Instead of

```
TO VAST? :N
IF ANYOF :N > 10000 :N < -10000 THEN
      OUTPUT "TRUE ELSE OUTPUT "FALSE
END
```

you can redefine it as

```
TO VAST? :N
TEST ANYOF :N > 10000 :N < -10000
IFTRUE OUTPUT "TRUE
IFFALSE OUTPUT "FALSE
END
```

The TEST command takes one input. TRUE or FALSE, and causes LOGO to note what it was. The IFTRUE command, IFT for short, causes the rest of the line to be obeyed only if the outcome of the previous TEST was TRUE. The IFFALSE command, IFF for short, works similarly.

Although TEST. IFTRUE and IFFALSE can make a procedure neater and more comprehensible, be careful with them. The TEST and the associated IFTRUE and/or IFFALSE must appear in the same procedure definition; you cannot have the IFTRUE or IFFALSE in a sub-procedure. Also, note that there is no point in having IFTRUE and IFFALSE on the same line; the commands after the first might be obeyed, but those after the second would never be.

---

1 If you are using Radio Shack LOGO or TI LOGO you can have many turtles without resorting to the device explained here.

3.7 **MORE ABOUT RECURSION**

Recursion, defining a procedure partly in terms of itself, is a very powerful technique and well worth mastering. It is not especially difficult to use and it can make many problems almost magically easy to solve. This section contains some examples and two or three simple rules of thumb for checking that you are getting it right.

Look at this:

```
TO JUNK
PRINT "HOHO
JUNK
END
```

It is recursive; if you run it HOHO will be repeatedly printed until you stop it. Make sure you know how to stop it, though if the worst comes to the worst you can always switch the machine off. In Terrapin LOGO the way to stop anything is to type CTRL-G (remember, that means press the CTRL key and then, while still pressing that, press G). The motto suggested by the JUNK procedure is that

Recursion can be an easy way to make something repeat indefinitely.

There are examples in earlier sections where this was or could have been applied, such as ANIMATE in section 3 and TICK in section 5.

Sometimes what a problem requires is repetition ending when some condition is satisfied, rather than repetition forever or for a known number of times. For instance, suppose that a problem requires that the turtle should move straight ahead until it reaches either side of the screen. The way to formalise what the turtle must do is

-    If at either side of the screen then do no more,

-    Otherwise FD 1 (or 5 or whatever is the chosen step size) and think again.

There is a Terrapin LOGO procedure called STOP which, like OUT-PUT, causes the procedure being run to finish at that point. If some other procedure called it, that one then resumes. STOP allows you to turn the plan above into LOGO:

```
TO TRUNDLE
IF ANYOF XCOR > 139 XCOR < -139 THEN STOP
FD 1
TRUNDLE
END
```

To see how this works, imagine that the turtle is at X=137.5, Y=0 (say) and its heading is 90 so that it is only three units from hitting the right-hand edge. If TRUNDLE is run, then

```
in line 1, the condition is not satisfied
so, line 2: the turtle moves FD 1 (now X=138.5)
line 3: TRUNDLE is obeyed ...
¦
¦   line 1: the condition is not satisfied, so
¦   line 2: the turtle moves FD 1 (now X=139.5)
¦   line 3: TRUNDLE is obeyed ...
¦   ¦
¦   ¦   line 1: the condition holds, so STOP
¦   ¦   causes this procedure to finish ...
¦   ¦
¦   ... and there is no more to do in this
¦   TRUNDLE, so it ends ...
¦
so the command is complete.
```

The turtle is at X=139.5, Y=0. True, this is not quite the edge of the screen, but you cannot have everything. TRUNDLE at least gets the turtle to within a 1 unit wide band at either side. To get it exactly to the edge there are only three possibilities:

(a)   Move it by 0.001 at a time. This is horribly slow.

(b)   Do some trigonometry. This is messy.

(c)   With no wrapping (after NOWRAP) try to send it past the edge. This causes an error, which stops everything and returns LOGO to waiting for your command.

None of these is entirely satisfactory; the unit-at-a-time way is a reasonable compromise. (Note for teachers: it would be possible to base a whole mathematics course on the art of reaching an acceptable compromise. LOGO would make a good vehicle for it.) The principle which TRUNDLE hints at is that

Recursion can be an easy way to cause repetition subject to some conditions.

3.7.1 Filling Areas With Colour

A very satisfying variation on the line drawings normally associated with LOGO is to have the turtle fill in whole areas on the screen. There are many ways to do this. As is often the case, one way is relatively easy and many are ghastly. An easy way is to imagine that the turtle is repeatedly drawing a line between its current position and some anchor point. To phrase it another way, imagine the turtle is anchored by an elastic thread to some point. As the turtle moves, what the thread sweeps over is filled in.

The SETXY command makes the turtle jump from one place to another, drawing a line in the current colour. Thus, to draw a line from its current place all it needs to do is to jump to the anchor point and then back to where it was. To turn this idea into LOGO, suppose that the X co-ordinate of the anchor point is stored as the value of a variable called ANCHORX, and the Y co-ordinate is similarly stored. There will need to be two more variables to record the turtle's proper position while it is at the anchor point: call them REALX and REALY. Then the following procedure is a sort of counterpoint to FD, which does what FD does but also fills in the area between the drawn line and the anchor point:

```
TO FILL.FD :N
IF :N=0 THEN STOP
MAKE "REALX XCOR
MAKE "REALY YCOR
SETXY :ANCHORX :ANCHORY
SETXY :REALX :REALY
FD 1
FILL.FD :N-1
END
```

It moves the turtle fairly slowly; hiding the turtle first (with HT) speeds it up a bit. To make it easy to shift the anchor point around, define

```
TO ANCHOR
MAKE "ANCHORX XCOR
MAKE "ANCHORY YCOR
END
```

Whenever ANCHOR is used, the turtle's current location becomes the anchor point. Figure 3.6 used FILL.FD and ANCHOR — it looks better in colour!

FILL.FD works because SETXY does not affect the turtle's heading, so when the second SETXY is done the turtle is back to

Figure 3.6

where it was when the procedure was started. Suppose that the IF command were left out. Then FILL.FD would invoke itself endlessly and the turtle would not stop moving until you typed CTRL-G, if it were being allowed to wrap. Therefore, obviously,

A recursive procedure which is not to run indefinitely must include some conditional command that may stop it. The conditional command must come **before** the recursive use of the procedure in the definition.

A basic safeguard is to check a recursive procedure by eye, and see what its inputs are used for. If the IF command were missing from FILL.FD, then the :N would not be used for anything other than part of the input to the final recursive use of FILL.FD, and that should at least arouse your suspicions.

3.7.2 Output By A Recursive Procedure

The overworked example used in 99% of all known programming books is the 'factorial' function, written

n!

and meaning the product of all the integers from 1 to n inclusive - so 3! is 6, and 4! is 24. Rather than spoil your expectations, here it is in LOGO – it is very concise:

```
TO FACTORIAL :N
IF :N=1 THEN OUTPUT 1 ELSE OUTPUT
     :N * FACTORIAL :N-1
END
```

This is based on the straightforward observation that if you know the product of the integers from 1 to :N-1 (which is FACTORIAL :N-1) then FACTORIAL :N is just :N times that. The observation transliterates readily into pseudo-LOGO as

```
FACTORIAL :N is :N * FACTORIAL :N-1
```

but this has no conditional command, so that recursion never stops. Recursion can only stop if at some point the procedure outputs the result of some expression which does not itself involve FACTORIAL. For example, you could always note that FACTORIAL 3 is 6, and begin the definition with

```
IF :N=3 THEN OUTPUT 6 ELSE ...
```

but then you would find, perhaps by experience (like everyone else), that it did not work if N was 1 or 2.

EXERCISES

(14)   What if N is not an integer?

A much less well-aired example is the finding of the cube root of a number. Although there is a cunning algorithm usable by someone who excels at mental arithmetic, it is somewhat elaborate and unnecessary when you have an obedient computer to do some brute calculations for you. The method to be applied here is the honourable and ancient mathematical one of inspired guesswork. Take an example: what is the cube root of 9? Clearly it lies between 1 and 9. Perhaps it is the average of 1 and 9, namely 5. No, 5 cubed is 125. Moreover, 1 cubed is 1, so it must lie between 1 and 5. Perhaps it is their average, 3? No, 3 cubed is 27, so it is between 1 and 3. Perhaps it is their average, 2? No, 2 cubed is only 8 so it must lie between 2 and 3 ... and so on. In theory this process never ends. However, LOGO cannot deal with more than seven significant digits in a number. When the calculation has reached seven digit accuracy then as far as LOGO is concerned the average is equal to one of the numbers – and that is when to stop. It would be a lot of effort if you were going to do it on paper, but it is no skin off your nose if it is LOGO that does the work. To formalise the method, define a procedure that has three inputs, namely the number whose cube root is to be found, a low guess and a high guess. Its title will be

```
TO CUBE.ROOT :N :LOW :HIGH
```

The first step is to average the guesses:

```
MAKE "AV ( :LOW + :HIGH ) / 2
```

If this is at the limit of accuracy, output it:

```
IF ANYOF :AV = :LOW :AV = :HIGH THEN
    OUTPUT :AV
```

If it is not then, if it is too high look again between :LOW and :AV, otherwise look again between :AV and :HIGH, like this:

```
IF :AV * :AV * :AV > :N THEN
    OUTPUT CUBE.ROOT :N :LOW :AV
    ELSE OUTPUT CUBE.ROOT :N :AV :HIGH
```

and that is all there is to it. If you are doubtful, try it and see. If it offends your eye to have to give three inputs then you can always beautify the whole affair this way:

```
TO CU.RT :N
OUTPUT CUBE.ROOT :N 1 :N
END
```

You should find this works surprisingly fast.

EXERCISES

(15)   Is it sensible to use the same method for fourth roots?

(16)   There is still a problem if the input to CU.RT is negative, or between 0 and 1. How can you fix it?

(17)   Why is the stopping test in CUBE.ROOT not :AV * :AV * :AV = :N ?

{18}   For keen mathematicians: define ARCSIN, the inverse of SIN.

3.8 DIAGRAMS DRAWN BY RECURSION

Many of the best mathematicians of all time have devoted a significant amount of their effort to studying figures drawn by essentially recursive methods. Although there are interesting theorems to be dug out, much of the motivation has been purely the beauty of the results. The power of LOGO makes the area readily accessible to your exploration.

To start with, consider the command FORWARD 90. The turtle, afterwards, is 90 units away but has the same heading. It is rather mundane for the turtle to get there along a straight line. Make it take a more devious route, such as that in figure 3.7. A procedure to do this, for any input as well as 90, is

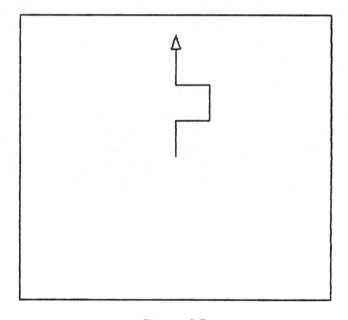

Figure 3.7

```
TO  DOODLE :N
FD :N / 3
RT  90  FD :N / 3
LT  90  FD :N / 3
LT  90  FD :N / 3
RT  90  FD :N / 3
END
```

This can be thought of as a 'more interesting' sort of FORWARD; it has the same overall effect on the turtle's state. Therefore, why not use it instead of FORWARD – in particular, inside the definition of DOODLE?

```
TO  DOODLE :N
DOODLE :N / 3
RT  90  DOODLE :N / 3
LT  90  DOODLE :N / 3
LT  90  DOODLE :N / 3
RT  90  DOODLE :N / 3
END
```

Either by looking at this, or by trying it, you ought to see that this is not quite good enough. The recursion never stops because there is no conditional command involved. To get round this, include at the start a command to say that if the input is suitably small then just do FORWARD rather than the fancy path:

```
IF :N < 5 THEN FD :N STOP
```

Remember, this has to come before the first recursive use of DOODLE in the definition. It is also a good idea to use a variable, say one called MIN, instead of 5. That way if 5 turns out to be not quite the right choice of a small number, you need only change the value of MIN rather than edit DOODLE. This is yet another application of the principle that you should really try to make things easy for yourself... Figure 3.8 shows the result of DOODLE 100.

Spend some time trying other variations, other choices for the indirect path to replace the straight line. But note: each segment of the path must be shorter than the whole. If not, the input to one of the DOODLEs in the definition will not be any smaller than the input to the main DOODLE, and so when it is run it will not be progressing towards the point at which the 'halt recursion' condition is satisfied. Apart from this, your most likely problem is to forget to include the STOP.

Here is a variant of the idea, shown in figure 3.9

```
TO  BRANCH :N
```

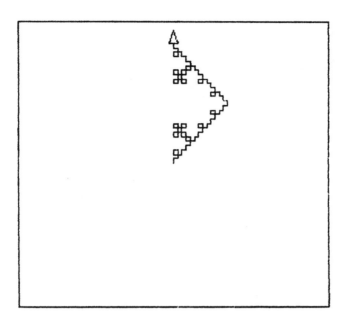

Figure 3.8

```
IF :N < 3 THEN STOP
FD :N
RT 45 BRANCH :N * 0.6
LT 90 BRANCH :N * 0.4
RT 45
BK :N
END
```

An interesting thing about this definition is that if the sub-procedures BRANCH :N * 0.6 and BRANCH :N * 0.4 are state-transparent, then the whole thing is. Now, certainly, if the input is very small (less than 3), BRANCH is state-transparent because all it does is STOP and nothing else. Having seen this, you can convince yourself that BRANCH is state-transparent whatever its input. Again there is a vast selection of variations on this idea, for example you can have three or more BRANCH commands within the definition. An area to experiment with is to see if a procedure can meaningfully be 'nearly but not quite' state-transparent – make the first line

```
IF :N < 3 THEN FD 1 STOP
```

and see what happens.

Finally, here, without further comment, is a famous example first suggested by the German mathematician David Hilbert:

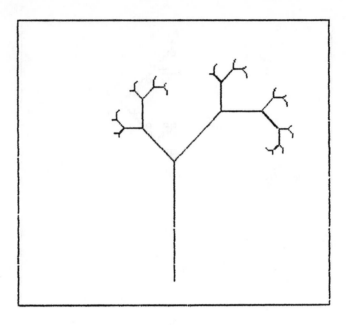

Figure 3.9

```
TO LHAND :S :N              TO RHAND :S :N
IF :N=0 THEN STOP          IF :N=0 THEN STOP
LT 90                          RT 90
RHAND :S :N - 1                LHAND :S :N - 1
FD :S                          FD :S
RT 90                      LT 90
LHAND :S :N - 1            RHAND :S :N - 1
FD :S                          FD :S
LHAND :S :N - 1            LHAND :S :N - 1
RT 90                      LT 90
FD :S                          FD :S
RHAND :S :N - 1                LHAND :S :N - 1
LT 90                          RT 90
END                        END
```

There is no accompanying diagram, you will just have to try it! To start with, try LHAND 30 2 and LHAND 18 3 with the turtle at the centre of the screen.

3.9 AFTERTHOUGHT

This chapter has provided you with nearly all the ingredients for some sort of 'turtle billiards'.

3.10 FILING AND OTHER CONVENIENCES

If you have worked through this chapter, you should now have several procedures, some of which are worth keeping for the future. Of course you may by this time have lost track of what you have defined. The way to find out what you have is to use the Terrapin LOGO procedure PRINTOUT, or PO for short. It expects one input, which can be

TITLES   The effect of

> PO TITLES

is to print, on the screen, the title line of each procedure you have defined (and not erased) in the current LOGO session. This is so useful that it can be further abbreviated to POTS.

NAMES   The effect of

> PO NAMES

is to print the name and value of each existing variable.

PROCEDURES
The effect of

> PO PROCEDURES

is to print out the title and definition of each procedure. It is not very useful, because everything tends to flash before your eyes on the screen. There is a mechanism explained in the technical manual that comes with Terrapin LOGO whereby whatever is printed on the screen can simultaneously be printed on a printer, if you have one.

a name   The name of a procedure (though without a quote); for instance,

> PO JUNK

would print the title and definition of JUNK, if it existed.

ALL   This prints everything – variables and procedures.

The procedure ERASE gets LOGO to discard a procedure. Normally the input is the name of a procedure, though without a quote. ERASE also accepts ALL, NAMES or PROCEDURES, just like PRINTOUT. (Note for teachers: ERASE, PRINTOUT, EDIT and TO are the only cases in Terrapin LOGO where the quote before the name is unreasonably omitted.) The procedure ERNAME can be used to get LOGO to discard its knowledge of a named variable – the input does take a quote mark beforehand.

It is possible to preserve a copy of all the current procedure definitions on a disk (if you are unsure about using a disk, check with the technical manual). The procedure is SAVE; it expects as its input a word by which you wish to name the whole collection of current procedures. For example,

    SAVE "MARCH.23.STUFF

In a similar fashion, you can save a picture by using SAVEPICT:

    SAVEPICT "MONA.LISA

To fetch a group of procedures from the disk at the start of the next session (or any other time), use READ. For example,

    READ "MARCH.23.STUFF

would fetch all the procedures you had previously saved with that SAVE command above. Any procedures existing before the READ in the current session will still exist, provided that their names were not the same as any of those procedures fetched by READ.

To fetch a picture from the disk, use READPICT:

    READPICT "MONA.LISA

This will destroy any current drawing. It will not affect the turtle, and in particular the turtle will not necessarily be where you left it when you did the SAVEPICT.

Eventually you will forget what is on the disk. Use CATALOG to find out; it takes no inputs and just causes the names of the various procedure collections and pictures to be printed. A procedure collection will have '.LOGO' after its name, and a picture will have '.PICT' after its name. If you want to throw away one or more of them (disks do have limited though large capacity) use ERASEFILE to get rid of a procedure collection or ERASEPICT to get rid of a picture. The commands

ERASEPICT "MONA.LISA

will irrevocably discard what had been saved under these names.
Here are some useful guidelines:

(a)   Make the names sensible. It might be fun to call some-
        thing RABBIT, but it is not very helpful a few days later.

(b)   At the end of a session, use POTS to check on what
        exists. Use ERASE to prune out unwanted procedures
        before using SAVE.

(c)   You can merge two SAVEd collections by READing in first
        one then the other, and then SAVEing the combined col-
        lection under a new name. If you use an existing name
        you will lose what was previously stored under that name.

(d)   There is no easy way to merge two pictures.

Chapter 4
Words and lists

Aims   Chapters 2 and 3 have been almost entirely concerned with graphics. This one is not. It has more to say about words, and it introduces a third kind of entity called lists. It also develops the idea of creating a 'toolkit' of procedures.

Note   Alas, Radio Shack Color LOGO does not have the features to be described in this chapter. If you are using this LOGO, you can skip chapters 4 and 5. You won't be able to tackle the majority of projects in chapter 7 either. However, Radio Shack Color LOGO does have some compensatory extras. The most exciting is that it allows you to use numerous turtles, which can send each other messages. Appendix D tells you more.

4.1 WORDS

Words in LOGO look similar to printed words in English, although they are not formed according to quite the same rules. In particular, there are precise rules in LOGO whereas in English rules, if they exist at all, are very flexible. LOGO words were introduced in chapter 2, as names of variables. A word in Terrapin LOGO is composed of any sequence of printable characters except for a space or a left or right square bracket (that is, '[' or ']'). Even these can be part of a word if you surround the whole word by single quote marks. Thus

WHO??	FATIMA
‹?.**	'LESSER FLAMINGO'
23907	PRICE.OF.BUTTER
PRINT	+
THIS.IS.A.LONGISH.WORD	

are all acceptable words. Three of these look like a number, a

LOGO procedure and an arithmetic operation. In general, the way to distinguish a word from something it might be confused with – such as the name of a not-yet-defined LOGO procedure – is to put a double quote mark before it[1]. So,

    PRINT FATIMA

will, in Terrapin LOGO, produce the error message

    THERE IS NO PROCEDURE NAMED FATIMA

whereas

    PRINT "FATIMA

will do just what it suggests. The initial quote mark, being an indication to LOGO, will not be printed, though

    PRINT ""FATIMA

will print "FATIMA rather than FATIMA. Similarly,

PRINT "PRICE.OF.BUTTER	prints	PRICE.OF.BUTTER
PRINT "<?.**	prints	<?.**
PRINT "'LESSER FLAMINGO'	prints	LESSER FLAMINGO
PRINT "239	prints	239
PRINT "PRINT	prints	PRINT
PRINT "+	prints	+

The PRINT "23 example is surprising. In fact, Terrapin LOGO is somewhat woolly-minded about the difference between numbers and words. In particular,

    PRINT "23 + 24

will print 47, but

    PRINT "23+24

will print 23+24 (and not 47) because now the whole group of characters after the quote cannot be a number because there is a plus sign in the middle of it. Terrapin LOGO does not object to you using the character '+' in the middle of a word. Moreover, a

---

1 Some LOGO systems, such as Research Machines LOGO, use a single quote, sometimes called an apostrophe, rather than the normal double inverted comma which most people would think was meant by the phrase "quote mark". If your LOGO system is one of those, then it probably has other and more restrictive rules about what is or is not a word.

word with only digits in it is still a perfectly good name for a variable:

    MAKE "2 397

Then

    PRINT 2   prints 2
    PRINT :2   prints 397

Also,

    PRINT :2 + 3

prints 400, but the command

    PRINT :2+3

produces the error message

    THERE IS NO NAME 2+3

meaning that there is no variable so named. You will find, in Terrapin LOGO, that the single quote is also a potential boobytrap. For example,

    PRINT "THAT'S

is legal and prints THAT'S, and indeed

    PRINT "'THATS ALL FOLKS

prints THATS ALL FOLKS because Terrapin LOGO tolerates not finding the matching single quote at the end of the line. It acts, reasonably, as though you had forgotten it or were too lazy to put it in. However,

    PRINT "'THAT'S ALL FOLKS

is not legal; you would be told

    THERE IS NO PROCEDURE NAMED S

To summarise, the rules are

    Use a double quote before a word, if it might be con-
    fused with something else (there is only one place where
    confusion cannot arise, and that is inside a list – see
    section 4 below).

Be careful about single quotes.

(Note for teachers: the idea of 'rule' is not the same as 'formal definition'. Where the formal definition is a mess, it is much better to give some examples and then emphasise that caution is needed.)

There is a procedure WORD? which takes one input, and outputs TRUE only if the input is a word. If you are in doubt, use it.

There is one unusual case worth knowing about, which follows from the definition. A word need have no characters at all! The command

    PRINT "

prints a blank line. This case is called the 'empty word'.

So far, all the printing has been one word per line, which is next to useless for practical purposes. To get round this, there is a version of PRINT called PRINT1. It behaves like PRINT except that it does not start a new line after printing its input(s). If you use only PRINT1 then the prompt which appears after the command has finished will appear on the same line as your printing. Here are some examples:

    PRINT1 "HELLO PRINT1 "THERE

prints HELLOTHERE and the next prompt appears immediately next to the final 'E'.

    PRINT1 "HELLO PRINT "THERE

prints HELLOTHERE and the next prompt will be on the line below. Notice that PRINT1 does not put any space after what it prints. To separate words by space you need quite explicitly to print a word consisting of spaces:

    PRINT1 "HELLO PRINT1 "' ' PRINT "THERE

prints HELLO THERE.

It can be very tedious to use one PRINT or PRINT1 command per word. As a convenience, Terrapin LOGO allows you to use just one PRINT or PRINT1 command for any number of inputs, provided that you surround the whole printing command with parentheses. Thus

    (PRINT "HELLO "THERE)

prints HELLO THERE. Beware, though, of the following mistake:

(PRINT "HELLO "THERE)

is an error because LOGO takes the second word to be 'THERE)' rather than 'THERE' and so cannot find the matching right parenthesis. Quite reasonably, on the other hand,

(PRINT 2 3)

prints 2 3.

The LOGO jargon used to describe a procedure such as PRINT which can take many inputs, is that it 'can be greedy'. In this book you have only met four procedures so far which can be greedy: PRINT, PRINT1, ALLOF and ANYOF. You will meet others in this chapter.

4.2 BEAUTIFUL PRINTING, PART 1

All this opens up the possibility of printing text on the screen in fancy ways. However, the effect of having an exotically printed display of information would be marred by having all those previous command lines on the screen. You can reset the displaying of text on the screen by using the procedure

CLEARTEXT

This wipes away all the text; the next prompt will appear at the top left of the area in which text can appear. If you specified DRAW recently, this means the twentieth line, first column. If you specified NODRAW recently, this means the top left of the screen. Note that CTRL-F, CTRL-S and CTRL-T do not affect this.

You can make printing appear where you like, within reason, by using the procedure CURSOR. This takes two numbers as inputs; the first is the column where printing is to start next, counting from column 0, and the second is the line number, counting from line 0. Column 0, line 0 is at the top left of the screen. The column must lie in the range 0 to 39, and the line number must be in the range 0 to 23. A further restriction is that CURSOR rounds its inputs to be integers, so you cannot use commands such as CURSOR 12.5 20.5 to produce fancy subscripts or superscripts.

Within these restrictions, CURSOR is very useful. For instance,

TO CRAWL
CURSOR 10 21

```
CURSOR 10 21
(PRINT1 "'X = ' XCOR )
CURSOR 10 22
(PRINT1 "'Y = ' YCOR )
FD 1
CRAWL
END
```

makes the turtle crawl along its current heading, while a display of its X and Y co-ordinates is continually updated. If the heading is not a multiple of 90 degrees the co-ordinates will have decimal parts, and the display will be changing so much that it is pretty confusing. It would be better to ROUND the co-ordinates first. If you edit CRAWL to be this,

```
TO CRAWL
CURSOR 10 21
(PRINT1 "'X = ' ROUND XCOR )
CURSOR 10 22
(PRINT1 "'Y = ' ROUND YCOR )
FD 1
CRAWL
END
```

you may be puzzled to find that sometimes either or both co-ordinates seem to be much too big. What is happening is this. Imagine that the X co-ordinate is just above 100, and decreasing. When it is 100 the number 100 will be printed starting at column 14 of line 21. When the X co-ordinate drops to around 99, the 99 will be printed starting at column 14 of line 21. However, 99 is only two digits long whereas 100 was three. The final 0 digit of 100 will not be overwritten when the 99 is printed, so the co-ordinate will appear on the screen to be 990. The cure is to print as many spaces after the number as are necessary to guarantee that the previous number is fully overwritten, for example

```
TO CRAWL
CURSOR 10 21
(PRINT1 "'X = ' ROUND XCOR "'   ' )
CURSOR 10 22
(PRINT1 "'Y = ' ROUND YCOR "'   ' )
FD 1
CRAWL
END
```

The CURSOR procedure was also used in this procedure to produce figure 4.1, with the command shown at the top left, previously defined.

```
?REBUS 0              ABRACADABRA
?                    ABRACADABRA
                    ABRACADABRA
                   ABRACADABRA
                  ABRACADABRA
                 ABRACADABRA
                ABRACADABRA
               ABRACADABRA
              ABRACADABRA
             ABRACADABRA
            ABRACADABRA
           ABRACADABRA
          ABRACADABRA
         ABRACADABRA
        ABRACADABRA
       ABRACADABRA
      ABRACADABRA
     ABRACADABRA
    ABRACADABRA
   ABRACADABRA
  ABRACADABRA
 ABRACADABRA
ABRACADABRA
```

Figure 4.1

4.3 NEW WORDS FROM OLD

There are times when, in a problem, you need to be able to assemble a word from some constituent parts. In Terrapin LOGO there is a procedure WORD which normally takes two inputs, though it can be greedy, and concatenates the characters of its inputs to form one larger word. The resulting word is output. An example:

```
PRINT WORD "CAN "DID
```

prints CANDID, and

```
MAKE "FATHER "DOMINIC
PRINT THING WORD "FAT "HER
```

prints DOMINIC. (Note: this is a case where the colon cannot be used in place of THING.) An example of greedy use is

```
PRINT (WORD "IN "TERM "IN "ABLE )
```

prints INTERMINABLE – do not forget the space before the right-hand parenthesis.

There are other circumstances for which WORD is useful, besides playing about with English words. One sometimes arises in large LOGO procedures when you need to use a substantial number of variables. You do not want to type in all their names, or perhaps you do not know how many will be needed when you are only at the stage of defining the procedures. However, you also want to be sure that none of the variables already exists, because if one did it might already be in active use for some other purpose. The variable named X, for instance, tends to be overused. The idea, then, is to define a procedure which generates, at each successive use, the next word in the sequence VAR1, VAR2, VAR3 ... provided that word is not already in use as the name of a variable. This procedure, say called GENVAR, will be used with MAKE, for instance

```
   ...
MAKE "NEWNAME GENVAR
MAKE :NEWNAME 87
   ...
```

The logical ingredients for defining GENVAR are

(a)   Get the next unused number in the sequence 1, 2, 3,. which could form part of the word to be output. The easy way to do this is to store it as the value of a variable, say GEN.NEXT, and increment its value each time GENVAR is used.

(b)   Concatenate 'VAR' and this number to form a possible word to output.

(c)   Use THING? to see if this word is the name of an existing variable. If not, output it. If it is, do all the steps again (by recursion?).

This translates fairly directly into LOGO as

```
MAKE "GEN.NEXT 0
TO GENVAR
MAKE "GEN.NEXT :GEN.NEXT + 1
TEST THING? WORD "VAR :GEN.NEXT
IFFALSE OUTPUT WORD "VAR :GEN.NEXT
IFTRUE OUTPUT GENVAR
END
```

There are interesting details in this procedure. The variable GEN.NEXT does not have to be incremented first of all, but it will have to be at some point and this way is neat (try it another way and see). You may also be surprised to see IFFALSE appearing before IFTRUE, but there is no reason why not. Because of this, the TEST/IFTRUE/IFFALSE method of defining conditionals is more flexible, although more verbose, than IF..THEN..ELSE. A third point to note in GENVAR is that the OUTPUT is needed in the last line. If you cannot see why, try the experiment of leaving it out.

GENVAR can be tested easily:

    MAKE "VAR3 "SOMETHING
    REPEAT 4 [PRINT GENVAR]

should print VAR1, VAR2, VAR4 and VAR5 because VAR3 is already in use.

4.4 LISTS

In addition to numbers and words, LOGO also deals with a third sort of entity, lists. These are the most versatile and elaborate of the three. A list is just an ordered collection of numbers, words and .. lists. The word 'ordered' means that it does matter which number, word or list in the collection comes first, which comes second and so on. A list is expressed in LOGO by writing the members of the collection in order and enclosing the whole lot in square brackets. For example,

    [23 6 1 99]

is a list with four members. The word 'element' is a common synonym for 'member'. Because a list is ordered, the list

    [23 1 6 99]

is not the same as the example above. Here are some more examples of lists:

[PIES 1 75]   This has three elements, a word and two
                   numbers.

[THIS IS A LIST]   This has four elements, all words.

[[0 0] [29 76]]   This has two elements. The first is the list [0 0]
                   and the second is the list [29 76].

[[[A Q] [R T]]]   This has one element, the list [[A Q] [R T]]
                   which itself has two elements.

[]   This has no elements at all. This is a very common example called the empty list.

Lists can be used to represent almost any kind of information, whether that information has some order to it or not. The first example above shows how a list might be used to represent pricing information. The second shows how a list can represent an English phrase or sentence. The third shows how a list might be used to represent a set of X and Y co-ordinate pairs.

Try PRINTing examples of lists. You will find that PRINT, in Terrapin LOGO at least, omits the outermost pair of square brackets[1], for example

```
PRINT [HELLO BOSS]          prints HELLO BOSS
PRINT [EH? [OUCH]]          prints EH? [OUCH]
PRINT [ ]                   prints a blank line
```

Try using lists as values for variables:

```
MAKE "TRY [THIS IS A TEST]
PRINT :TRY
```

will print THIS IS A TEST. You will find that you are never obliged to separate a square bracket from anything else by spaces, though you can if you like.

You should now see that the REPEAT command, introduced in chapter 2, just takes two inputs. The first is a number, the second is a list representing an ordered sequence of commands. Therefore

```
MAKE "X [FD RANDOM 30 RT 90]
REPEAT 5 :X
.. move the turtle ..
REPEAT 3 :X
.. move the turtle ..
REPEAT 12 :X
.. etc ..
```

saves a lot of repetitive typing.

A list can never be mistaken for the name of a procedure to be run; procedure names must always be words. Because of this, words do not need an initial double quote when they are used within a list. Consider this faulty pair of commands:

---

1 If you want, you can change this. See the Terrapin LOGO technical manual for details.

```
MAKE "X 100
PRINT [:X IS 100]
```

This does not print [100 IS 100]. Because the ':X' is within a list,
LOGO treats it just as a word rather than 'the value of the variable called X'. Remember that ':X' is a legal possibility for a
word, for instance

```
MAKE "Y "':X'
PRINT :Y
```

prints :X. But note, REPEAT treats lists as commands.

4.5 USING LISTS

4.5.1 Informative Messages

In the factorial procedure in section 3.7.2, it was assumed that
the input was a positive integer. If it was 0 or negative the procedure recursed happily until stopped by CTRL-G. If the input was
not a number but a word, Terrapin LOGO would give the unap-
petising message

```
= DOESNT LIKE word AS INPUT, IN LINE
IF :N=1 THEN OUTPUT 1 ELSE OUTPUT :N
* FACTORIAL :N-1
AT LEVEL 1 OF FACTORIAL
```

(Note that the phrase 'AT LEVEL 1' means that there was only
one procedure – FACTORIAL – which had started but had not finished when the error occurred.) You can make your assumptions
about FACTORIAL explicit by introducing some conditional commands to check that the input is what you intended:

```
TO FACTORIAL :N
IF WORD? :N THEN PRINT [WORD INPUT
      TO FACTORIAL] STOP
IF :N<1 THEN PRINT [INPUT LESS THAN
      1] STOP
IF :N=1 THEN OUTPUT 1 ELSE OUTPUT
      :N * FACTORIAL :N-1
END
```

Here lists are used to provide short informative messages to make
the procedure more foolproof. Alas, it is still not perfect. Consider
the command

```
PRINT FACTORIAL 2.5
```

The procedure FACTORIAL 2.5 will try to output 2.5 * FACTORIAL 1.5. The procedure FACTORIAL 1.5 will try to output 1.5 * FACTORIAL 0.5. The procedure FACTORIAL 0.5 will print INPUT LESS THAN 1 and stop, not outputting anything. Thus the expression 1.5 * FACTORIAL 0.5 will be an error - Terrapin LOGO will tell you that

```
FACTORIAL DIDNT OUTPUT, IN LINE
IF :N=1 THEN OUTPUT 1 ELSE OUTPUT :N
* FACTORIAL :N-1
AT LEVEL 2 OF FACTORIAL
```

(Here it is 'AT LEVEL 2' because FACTORIAL 2.5 had started but not finished; it was waiting for the output from FACTORIAL 1.5 which had started but had not finished when the error was encountered.) All this tends to spoil the hoped-for simplicity of the informative message.

As is so often the case, there is an easy repair. There is a procedure TOPLEVEL which, like STOP, immediately ends the procedure it appears within. Unlike STOP, it ends every other unfinished procedure as well, so that LOGO immediately returns to waiting for your next command. Putting a TOPLEVEL at some point in a procedure is very much like telling LOGO "imagine I type a CTRL-G at this point". The repair to FACTORIAL is to use TOPLEVEL instead of STOP. Indeed, because of what TOPLEVEL does, you can define a generally useful procedure called ERROR which takes one input - usually to be a list - and use it in conditional commands that check for errors:

```
TO ERROR :MESSAGE
PRINT :MESSAGE
TOPLEVEL
END

TO FACTORIAL :N
IF WORD? :N THEN ERROR [WORD INPUT TO
    FACTORIAL]
IF :N<1 THEN ERROR [INPUT LESS THAN 1]
    .. etc ..
```

A procedure such as ERROR is a very useful tool. You may wonder, why is it not provided as standard? Fundamentally the answer is that LOGO is really a kit of useful procedures from which to assemble procedures to suit your own particular needs. ERROR, taking only one input, could be too specific for some purposes. For example, you might choose to start each session of LOGO with

```
    MAKE "ERROR.COUNT 0
```

and define ERROR as

```
    TO ERROR :MESSAGE
    PRINT :MESSAGE
    MAKE "ERROR.COUNT :ERROR.COUNT + 1
    PRINT1 [THAT WAS BLUNDER NUMBER]
    PRINT1 "' '
    PRINT :ERROR.COUNT
    TOPLEVEL
    END
```

The aim of LOGO's designers has been to provide a collection of procedures which was sufficiently general and yet sufficiently complete for users to put it to a very wide variety of uses.

4.5.2 Constructing Lists From Bits

Wide though the possibilities suggested by this last section are, it is ultimately limiting if every list used in any procedure is one that had to be typed in at some point. LOGO provides ways of assembling lists from bits, and for turning sentences typed by you into lists. For the latter, Terrapin LOGO provides REQUEST, or RQ for short. REQUEST takes no input; it waits till the user has typed a line, and then outputs that line as a list:

```
    TO HELLO
    PRINT1 [WHO ARE YOU]
    MAKE "REPLY REQUEST
    (PRINT1 "'HELLO ' :REPLY)
    END
```

If you give the command HELLO you might see something like this on your screen:

```
    ?HELLO
    WHO ARE YOU?ATTILA THE HUN
    HELLO ATTILA THE HUN
    ?
```

Terrapin LOGO also provides two procedures for constructing lists:

LIST   This takes two inputs normally, though it can be greedy.
            It outputs a list formed from its inputs

SENTENCE This procedure, SE for short, also takes two inputs normally and can also be greedy. It too outputs a list formed from its inputs. However, if any input is a list it first breaks it up into its elements, for example [THIS LIST] would be treated as the two words THIS LIST. It does not do this recursively; lists within lists are not broken up.

Some examples should help:

    LIST "HELLO "SIR

outputs [HELLO SIR].

    LIST 2*5 "COMMANDMENTS

outputs [10 COMMANDMENTS].

    (LIST [HO HO] "HE "SAID)

outputs [[HO HO] HE SAID].

    (LIST 1 2 3 4 5)

outputs [1 2 3 4 5].

    SE "MICHAEL "MOUSE

outputs [MICHAEL MOUSE].

    (SE [HO HO] "HE "SAID)

outputs [HO HO HE SAID].

    SE [WHAT IS] [THE QUESTION]

outputs [WHAT IS THE QUESTION].

A simple mnemonic is that LIST puts square brackets around the collection of its inputs, and SENTENCE strips the outer square brackets off any of its inputs before putting square brackets around the lot.

As the names suggest, SENTENCE is the more useful in applications where lists are to be used essentially as sentences. LIST is often the more useful in other cases. As an example of the former here is a simple and educationally hopeless quiz procedure:

```
TO QUIZ
MAKE "N1 RANDOM 50
MAKE "N2 RANDOM 50
```

```
PRINT1 (SE [WHAT IS] :N1 "TIMES :N2 )
IF (SE :N1 * :N2 ) = REQUEST THEN
    PRINT [YES] ELSE PRINT SE [SHAME
    IT WAS] :N1 * :N2
QUIZ
END
```

It is educationally useless because if you give any wrong answer at all it tells you the correct answer! Note the line

```
IF (SE :N1 * :N2 ) = REQUEST THEN ...
```

SE has only one input, so (SE :N1 * :N2) is just the list whose sole element is the right answer. The REQUEST outputs a list formed from what the user types. If he types the right answer and nothing extra, the two lists will be equal.

As an example of using LIST, here is a simple fault-tracing aid called CHECK. Its input is assumed to be a word which is the name of a variable:

```
TO CHECK :QXRZ
PRINT (LIST :QXRZ "HAS "VALUE THING
    :QXRZ )
END
```

It can be used like this:

```
...
MAKE "X [120 110]
...
CHECK "X                          (Note, not CHECK :X)
```

- it will print

```
X HAS VALUE [120 110]
```

CHECK could be used within a procedure to print the values of the inputs if you were not sure what was going on and needed to make some basic checks. If SENTENCE were used here instead of LIST then CHECK would have printed the more confusing message

```
X HAS VALUE 120 110
```

The input to CHECK was called QXRZ because the name is unlikely to be used elsewhere. The name must be an unlikely one:

```
CHECK "QXRZ
```

will print QXRZ HAS VALUE QXRZ, which is true but unhelpful if you want to examine the value of some other variable called QXRZ.

TI LOGO does not have LIST, it only provides SENTENCE.

4.5.3 Dissecting Lists

LOGO also provides procedures for getting at bits of lists. In Terrapin LOGO there are four:

FIRST   This takes a list as input, and outputs the first element. Obviously, the input list must not be the empty list.

BUTFIRST This procedure, BF for short, takes a list as input and outputs a list formed by removing the first element. The input must not be the empty list. If the input list has only one element then the output list will be the empty list.

LAST   This is the opposite of FIRST. It takes a list as input, and outputs the last element. The input list must not be empty.

BUTLAST This procedure, BL for short, is the opposite of BUTFIRST. It outputs a list consisting of all but the last element of the input. The input list must not be empty.

These four procedures can also accept a word as input, and do the corresponding action with the first or last character of the word. Examples:

FIRST [HELLO SIR]	outputs HELLO
BF [HELLO SIR]	outputs [SIR]
FIRST "HELLO	outputs H
BF "HELLO	outputs ELLO
LAST [ONE TWO THREE]	outputs THREE
BUTLAST [ONE TWO THREE]	outputs [ONE TWO]
LAST "CLAMP	outputs P
BUTLAST "CLAMP	outputs CLAM

There is also a procedure LIST? which outputs TRUE or FALSE depending on whether its single input is a list or not.

It may seem perverse that there is no way directly to get hold of the second element of a list, or to replace the seventh (or whichever) element by something else. It **is** perverse. Failing to provide some such procedures is taking the aims of generality too far, especially since it is not a wholly trivial task to define them for yourself. There is a historical reason for it, but it is no longer valid. It was this: LOGO is descended from the language LISP. In LISP and in LOGO, there was and still is a commonplace requirement to be able to compare two lists. LISP users also frequently wanted to be able to make more elaborate checks, such as 'is [A B C D] a list containing only letters of the alphabet?'. In the early days of LISP, both software and hardware ideas were much less sophisticated. In particular it was conceptually more taxing, although not impossible, to handle whole entities such as lists where the size was unknown in advance. It was much easier, and mathematically more satisfying, to look on a list as though it had precisely two constituents – a 'first element' and a list, which was the BUTFIRST bit. In those terms the list

[A B C D]

might have been written as

(A, (B, (C, (D, ())))))

However the square bracket notation, or an equivalent of it, was adopted instead, being much easier to read and write. Unfortunately for you, the notation disguised the fact that a list really had exactly two constituents. Since those days both hardware and software science have made a lot of progress. Now, various versions of LOGO do provide procedures which allow you to deal directly with elements other than the first or last of a list. Terrapin LOGO, for compactness, has only provided LAST and BUTLAST as the symmetrical counterparts of FIRST and BUTFIRST. Anything beyond these you must create for yourself.

This brings out the notion of building yourself general toolkits of procedures. It is almost always much easier to step from a general case to a specific one than it is to do the reverse. This is because moving from the specific to the general requires you to articulate what the generalisation is, each time; in the other direction no such articulation is needed. The next section and its subsections are concerned with defining a small but very useful kit of tools for working with procedures. You would be well advised to spend one whole LOGO session working through it, so that at the end you could SAVE all the procedures as one collection (as a file) called, say, LISTSTUFF. Then in future, when you want to work with lists, you can ease the burden by giving a command

READ "LISTSTUFF

at the start.

4.5.4 What Is Needed?

When you embark on the construction of such a toolkit, the first step is to plan what will be in it. Remember that it is always possible to add to the collection at a later date. It is also very sensible not to let the size of the collection get out of hand. The planning usually demands imagination and some past experience of what is useful, and takes hours or days rather than minutes. If at this point you have not spent much time playing with lists in LOGO then the following thoughts should be helpful. They might also serve to set you thinking about some involved projects to do with lists.

Needs:

- It is useful to be able to test whether something is a member of a specified list. Suppose a procedure asked a question; the user could reply 'I THINK YES' or 'YES PERHAPS' or 'MY ANSWER IS YES' or 'YES INDEED' as well as plain 'YES'. If you used REQUEST to capture the answer, it would be nice to check whether YES was part of it. This could go wrong, the user might answer 'CERTAINLY NOT YES', but it is impossible to cater for every possibility.

- It is useful to be able to find out how many elements there are in a list (and how many characters there are in a word).

- It is useful to be able to get hold of the N-th element of a list, for any specified number N. Suppose you are working on devising LOGO procedures to encode or decode a message. The procedures FIRST, BUTFIRST, LAST and BUTLAST let you get at the characters in a word. You could create variables called A to Z, with values 1 to 26. Then, to encode a letter, say R, you need only look up the :R-th element of some predefined 'coding list', and let that stand for the letter R.

It is useful to be able to update one particular element of a list. Imagine your aim is to devise LOGO procedures to play tic-tac-toe, otherwise known as noughts-and-crosses. You could represent the state of play as a list with nine elements, for example

[BLANK X X BLANK O BLANK O BLANK BLANK]

to represent figure 4.2. If the 'O' player were to play in the top left cell, you would have to update the first element of the list from BLANK to O. (Note for those interested in the ideas of artificial intelligence: it is much harder to devise a procedure which plays badly but believably than it is to devise one which plays perfectly.) As another example, suppose you wanted to count letter frequencies in text typed by a user. You could represent the count for each character as one element of a large list. Each time a letter appeared you could make the corresponding element one larger than before. This is easier than having one variable per character because there are at least 57 likely characters, excluding lower case letters. There is a procedure ASCII which expects a one letter word as input and outputs a number which uniquely stands for that letter. The correspondence between numbers and characters is defined by the American Standard Code for Information Interchange – ASCII for short. Incidentally there is a procedure CHAR which does just the reverse. The Terrapin LOGO procedure READCHARACTER, RC for short, outputs a single

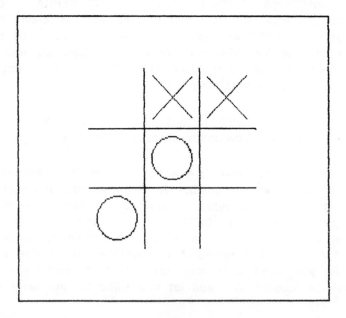

Figure 4.2

character word representing one keystroke by the user; you can type a certain number of characters ahead of a program that uses RC, and the LOGO system will preserve them so that RC can catch up. The procedure RC? outputs TRUE if there are any characters currently available for RC to read without waiting for the user's next character to be typed.

- It is useful to be able to construct a list consisting of all the elements common to two lists. Suppose that you are using LOGO to experiment with set theory and you are representing sets by lists. The 'intersection of two sets' will be the list of elements common to the two lists.

- It is useful to be able to construct a set which contains any element in either of two lists, but only once. In set theory this would be the union of two sets.

- It is useful to be able to generate a new list from a given one, in which every occurrence of some specified element has been replaced by a new element. An example of this will be given in chapter 7, in a project to create a simple database of facts.

This forms an adequate basic collection. In due course you will think of some others which are worth including, but remember to keep notes of what they do and what they do not do.

Is something in a list?

If you do not see at once how to define this, try an example: how can you test whether B is a member of [A B C]? The chief tools at your disposal are FIRST and BUTFIRST. Is B the FIRST of this list? No. Now you only have BUTFIRST left in your toolbag! The BUTFIRST of the list is [B C], and B is the FIRST of that. This suggests the following algorithm:

(a)   Is the something in question equal to the FIRST of the list? If so, output TRUE.

(b)   If not, is it a member of the BUTFIRST of the list?

The algorithm is not quite complete: so far there is no way it can output FALSE, yet it must be capable of doing so. The time to output FALSE is when there are no elements left to check – that is, when left with the empty list. Turning this into LOGO gives

```
TO MEMBER? :EL :L
IF :L = [] THEN OUTPUT "FALSE
IF :EL = FIRST :L THEN OUTPUT "TRUE ELSE
     OUTPUT MEMBER? :EL (BUTFIRST :L)
END
```

(the parentheses here are only for legibility). Test it.

Counting the number of elements

Again, the basic tools you have are FIRST and BUTFIRST. FIRST tells you what the first element is, but that does not help you to find out how many elements there are. Presumably, the main tool is therefore BUTFIRST. Consider an example: [A B C] has three elements. The BUTFIRST of it is [B C], which has two. So [A B C] has one more than the BUTFIRST of it has. What if the list is empty? Then, the count is zero. All this suggests this LOGO procedure:

```
TO COUNT :LIST
IF :LIST = [] THEN OUTPUT 0
OUTPUT 1 + COUNT BUTFIRST :LIST
END
```

Simple variations are possible. In particular, you can make COUNT work for words as well as lists:

```
TO COUNT :LIST
IF ANYOF :LIST = [] :LIST = " THEN OUTPUT 0
OUTPUT 1 + COUNT BUTFIRST :LIST
END
```

You might want to go back and extend MEMBER? in a similar way.

Getting the N-th element

If N is 1 it is easy – output the FIRST of the list. If N is not one, what is wanted is the (N-1)-th element of the BUTFIRST of the list. In LOGO:

```
TO ITEM :NTH :LIST
IF :NTH = 1 THEN OUTPUT FIRST :LIST
OUTPUT ITEM :NTH - 1 (BUTFIRST :LIST )
END
```

This is capable of improvement – what if :NTH is zero or

negative, or the list is too short? Here is a better version:

```
TO ITEM :NTH :LIST
IF ANYOF (:NTH < 1) (:LIST=[]) THEN
      ERROR [MISTAKE USING ITEM]
IF :NTH = 1 THEN OUTPUT FIRST :LIST
OUTPUT ITEM :NTH - 1 (BUTFIRST :LIST )
END
```

This uses the ERROR procedure defined in section 4.5.1. The procedure can also be extended so that it works with words and outputs the N-th character[1].

Updating an element of a list

Terrapin LOGO provides two procedures which are really specialised and restricted forms of SENTENCE. One, FPUT (an acronym for FirstPUT), is for glueing some element onto the front of a list. It takes two inputs, the second of which must be a list, and outputs a list whose first element is the first input and whose remainder is the second input, for example

```
FPUT "A [B C]
```

outputs [A B C]. The other procedure, LPUT (an acronym for Last-PUT), works in a predictably similar way. You can safely opt to forget about both of these; however, for the sake of showing them in use they will both be used in the remainder of this chapter.

When updating an element of a list you need to know three things: what the list is, which is the element to update and what its new value is to be. Again it is best to think about the simplest case first of all. To update the first element of a list, just output the list formed by glueing the new value onto the front of the BUTFIRST of the given list (that is, prune off the old value, glue on the new). If it is not the first element that is to be updated then it becomes a matter of updating the (N-1)-th element of the BUTFIRST of the given list, for instance to update the third element of [A B C D], update the second of [B C D]. Forethought, or one or two misfiring experiments, will remind you that it is also necessary to glue the FIRST element of the given list onto the result of updating the BUTFIRST of it.

This is the bones of it in LOGO:

```
TO UPDATE :N :LIST :NEW
```

1 In Apple LOGO and some others ITEM is provided for you.

```
IF :N = 1 THEN OUTPUT (FPUT :NEW
    BUTFIRST :LIST )
OUTPUT (FPUT (FIRST :LIST ) (UPDATE
    (:N - 1) BUTFIRST :LIST :NEW )
END
```

Once more, it makes sense to put in a first line similar to that included in ITEM above. (Note for teachers: the inputs to UPDATE appear in the order shown for a good reason, namely that it makes the use of UPDATE easier to verbalise. The expression UPDATE 2 [A B C] "Z could be read as 'update the second element of [A B C] to be Z'. It pays to get your students into this habit.)

Since both FPUT and SENTENCE always output a list, it is trickier to make UPDATE work for words too. It is undoubtedly neater to define a whole new procedure if you want to be able to do this operation on words. The corresponding procedure to FPUT or SENTENCE is WORD.

The intersection of two lists

Consider some examples: the intersection of [A B C] and [C A R] ought to be [C A] or [A C]. The intersection of [A B] and [C D] ought to be the empty list. It is reasonably clear that the thing to do is to work through the first list, and include each element that also features in the second list in the answer. Yet again, the tools for working through the first list are FIRST and BUTFIRST. To check whether an element features in the second list, you now have MEMBER? available. The only time that the answer is the empty list is when you have checked all the elements of the first list and are left with an empty first list.

In LOGO this could be expressed as

```
TO INTERSECT :L1 :L2
IF :L1 = [] THEN OUTPUT []
TEST MEMBER? (FIRST :L1 ) :L2
IFTRUE OUTPUT FPUT (FIRST :L1 )
    INTERSECT (BF :L1 ) :L2
IFFALSE OUTPUT INTERSECT (BF :L1 ) :L2
END
```

This may be the first time you have seen a procedure which invokes itself recursively in one of two possible places in its definition, rather than in just one possible place. If you are in doubt, try it out. It may help to work through an example on paper first.

The union of two lists

The union of [A B] and [A C] ought to be [A B C] or some permutation of it, rather than [A A B C]. The union of [A B] and [C] ought to be [A B C] or some permutation of that. The important point is to avoid unnecessary duplication of elements in the answer. As with INTERSECT the obvious method is to work through the first list, using FIRST and BUTFIRST. If the first list is empty the answer is just the second list, even if that is empty. If the first list is not empty, consider its first element. If it features in the second list, ignore it because that would otherwise lead to duplication. If it is not in the second list, glue it onto the union of the BUTFIRST of the first list, and the second list.

In LOGO this could be expressed in a manner very like the example of INTERSECT:

```
TO UNION :L1 :L2
IF :L1 = [] THEN OUTPUT :L2
TEST MEMBER? (FIRST :L1 ) :L2
IFTRUE OUTPUT UNION (BF :L1 ) :L2
IFFALSE OUTPUT FPUT (FIRST :L1 ) UNION
     (BF :L1 ) :L2
END
```

Compare this carefully with INTERSECT; the similarities are surprising.

Replacing all occurences of an element

Once more, the tools for working through the list are FIRST and BUTFIRST. If the list is empty, output the empty list. Otherwise, look at the first element. If it is an occurrence of what is to be replaced, use FPUT to put the new value onto the front of the result of processing the rest of the list. If not, FPUT the first element instead. In LOGO this is

```
TO REPLACE :OLD :NEW :L
IF :L = [] THEN OUTPUT []
TEST :OLD = FIRST :L
IFTRUE OUTPUT FPUT :NEW REPLACE
     :OLD :NEW (BF :L )
IFFALSE OUTPUT FPUT FIRST :L
     REPLACE :OLD :NEW (BF :L )
END
```

EXERCISES

If you have worked carefully through this chapter you should be able, with care and perhaps one or two false starts, to do these exercises. They are hard. Do not expect to do them in a few minutes. If you have not been following this chapter you are now on your own ...

(1)   Devise a procedure REVERSE that outputs a list formed by reversing its input:

    REVERSE [A B C]   should output [C B A]

(Hint: LPUT might help.)

(2)   Devise a procedure REVWORD that reverses a word:

    REVWORD "STRAP   should output PARTS

(3)   Devise a procedure which tests whether a word or a list is palindromic, that is, reads the same backwards as forwards. Try to do it more directly than by using the results of the first two exercises.

    PALINDROME "REFER   should output TRUE
    PALINDROME [A B B A]   should output TRUE
    PALINDROME [A B A B]   should output FALSE

(4)   Devise a procedure which prints out a list reasonably elegantly. What this means is for you to decide. As a suggestion, printing out the list

    [HERE [WITH [A FEW] FRILLS] IS A LIST]

might be nicely printed as

    HERE
            WITH
                    A
                    FEW
            FRILLS
    IS
    A
    LIST

Remember the procedure LIST? which tests whether its input is a list or not; it is analogous to WORD? and NUMBER?.

4.6 LISTS AND TURTLE GRAPHICS

Putting together your knowledge of lists and your knowledge of turtle graphics can expand your programming horizons considerably. Chapter 5 is largely concerned with a project in this area; chapter 7 suggests several others. This section describes two small projects for the sake of demonstrating some basic practical uses of lists.

4.6.1 Playing With Scale

This project was originally motivated by the idle thought that it would be fun to be able to shrink or enlarge shapes easily, and to turn them over. One way is to edit a procedure such as

```
TO BOX
REPEAT 4 [FD 100 RT 90]
END
```

so that it has an input, which is used as a multiplying factor for the 100. This permits change of scale, but not turning over.

What is involved in turning over a shape? Some playing about with simple non-symmetric shapes ought to convince you that what is needed is to replace FORWARD by BACKWARD and RIGHT by LEFT, and vice-versa. BACKWARD 100 is just the same as FORWARD -100, and LEFT 90 is the same as RIGHT -90. So, all that is needed is to reverse the signs of the numbers involved. The awkward point about this is that the definition of BOX will come to look cumbersome – it will need two inputs, one for the side length and one for the angle. It will also be an unreasonable amount of work to incorporate this feature in each new shape, and this would stop the whole enterprise from being fun or easy.

There is another approach. The key idea – which you may not feel is the best or even much use, but this is only a demonstration – is to represent simple shapes as lists of lists. Each list will contain two numbers, an amount to go FORWARD and an amount to turn RIGHT. For instance, the basic BOX would be

[[100 90] [100 90] [100 90] [100 90]]

It must be possible to define a procedure, say called DO, which takes such a list as input and draws the shape. The steps involved are:

(a)   If the list is empty just STOP.

(b)   Otherwise look at the FIRST of it (in the case of the box its [100 90]). Go FORWARD by the FIRST of this, turn RIGHT by the second element.

(c)   Now just DO the BUTFIRST of the list of lists.

Here is the LOGO definition:

```
TO DO :LL
IF :LL = [] THEN STOP
FORWARD FIRST (FIRST :LL )
RIGHT ITEM 2 (FIRST :LL )
DO BUTFIRST :LL
END
```

It is easy to give DO a second input which will be a scale factor:

```
TO DO :LL :SCALE
IF :LL = [] THEN STOP
FD :SCALE * FIRST (FIRST :LL )
RT ITEM 2 (FIRST :LL )
DO (BUTFIRST :LL ) :SCALE
END
```

To draw the shape turned over, use a separate procedure:

```
TO FLIP :LL :SCALE
IF :LL = [] THEN STOP
BK :SCALE * FIRST (FIRST :LL )
LT ITEM 2 (FIRST :LL )
FLIP (BUTFIRST :LL ) :SCALE
END
```

The beauty of DO and FLIP is that it is easy to express shapes as lists of lists. These two procedures could form the basis of a simple kit for experimenting with rotations and reflections.

4.6.2 Simple Shape Recording

When playing with SETX, SETY and SETXY, it often happens that you give values which are not quite correct and this mars the drawing. Either you accept the blemish or you start again. What motivates this project is the thought that it would be useful to be able to manoeuvre the turtle into the right spot, making mistakes on the way, and then record the spot somehow. Then it would be easy to clear the screen and draw a perfect shape by replaying the recording.

The main idea is to have a variable, say called RECORDING, whose value will be a list of lists each containing the X and Y co-ordinates of one spot. A procedure RECORD will be used to append the turtle's current co-ordinates to the end of the recording and update RECORDING. Another procedure, REPLAY, will be used to replay the recording. RECORD will only be used when the turtle is on a wanted spot.

RECORD is simple:

```
TO RECORD
MAKE RECORDING LPUT (LIST XCOR YCOR )
      :RECORDING
END
```

REPLAY is only slightly harder. You only need to SETXY to the co-ordinates given by the FIRST of RECORDING, then REPLAY the BUTFIRST of it. However, it would be pleasing if REPLAY took no inputs at all. It ought not to change RECORDING itself, because then you could only use REPLAY once. Here is one solution: use a subprocedure with an input.

```
TO REPLAY
PU SETXY (ITEM 1 FIRST :RECORDING )
      (ITEM 2 FIRST :RECORDING ) PD
PLAYBACK :RECORDING
END

TO PLAYBACK :L
IF :L = [] THEN STOP
SETXY (ITEM 1 FIRST :L ) (ITEM 2
      FIRST :L )
PLAYBACK BUTFIRST :L
END
```

The first line in REPLAY gets the turtle to the staring position; therefore it would be slightly more economical if the second line were PLAYBACK BF :RECORDING instead. Before trying the procedures, remember to

```
MAKE "RECORDING []
```

at the start.

4.6.3 The State Of The Turtle

If you want to play about with other such projects it may help you to know that Terrapin LOGO provides a procedure called TURTLE-STATE, or TS for short. It takes no input, and outputs a list of four elements:

- The first is TRUE if the pen is down, FALSE if not.

- The second is TRUE if the turtle is normally visible, FALSE if HIDETURTLE was last specified.

- The third is a number giving the background colour.

- The fourth is a number giving the pen colour.

This procedure together with XCOR, YCOR and HEADING tells you all there is to know about the state of the turtle at any time.

4.7 TWO NON-GRAPHIC EXAMPLES

This section gives two examples of the use of lists. The comments are brief.

4.7.1 A Calculator

This section describes a simple set of procedures which together form a 'reverse Polish' calculator, mimicing the way some pocket calculators work. The name 'reverse Polish' refers to a particular notation for arithmetic. Instead of expressing the product of 23 and 34 as

```
23 * 34
```

the 'reverse Polish' form is

```
23 34 *
```

that is, you enter the number 23 first, then the number 34, and only then do you say what is to be done with them – in this example, they are to be multiplied together. The principle behind the notation is that you are working with an ordered sequence of numbers, initially empty. Any number you enter is appended at the end of the sequence. If you specify an arithmetic operation it is carried out using the last (that is, most recent) two numbers of the sequence; those numbers are deleted from the end of the sequence by the operation, and the result is put there instead. Therefore you need to keep in mind what the sequence is. For example:

```
                        sequence: nothing
enter: 7                .. sequence: 7
enter: 9                .. sequence: 7 9
enter: 6                .. sequence: 7 9 6
enter: *                .. sequence: 7 54
enter: +                .. sequence: 61
enter: +                .. error! There is only one number.
```

The sequence will be stored in LOGO as a list, the value of a variable called SEQ. The main work will be done by a procedure R.POLISH, which will use REQUEST to get a number or an operation from the user. If it is a number it will be appended to the list, otherwise the appropriate operation will be done. It is convenient to have a fifth operation called 'P' which prints the sequence, and to have the last number in the sequence printed whether you specify a number or an operation.

In the definitions below, the procedure PUT puts its input onto the end of the sequence and the procedure GET takes one number off the end and outputs the number. The effect of the operation of addition is therefore just PUT (GET + GET). The definitions are

```
TO CALC
SETUP
R.POLISH
END

TO SETUP
MAKE "SEQ []
END

TO R.POLISH
PRINT1"'>> ' MAKE "IN REQUEST
IF (COUNT :IN ) > 1 THEN PRINT [ALL BUT
      FIRST ITEM IGNORED]
MAKE "IN FIRST :IN
IF NUMBER? :IN THEN PUT :IN
IF :IN = "* THEN PUT (GET * GET )
IF :IN = "/ THEN PUT (GET / GET )
IF :IN = "- THEN PUT (GET - GET )
```

```
IF :IN = "+ THEN  PUT (GET + GET )
IF :IN = "Q THEN  PRINT [QUIT] TOPLEVEL
IF :IN = "P THEN  PRINT :SEQ ELSE PRINT
     LAST :SEQ
R.POLISH
END

TO GET
MAKE "VAL LAST :SEQ
MAKE "SEQ BUTLAST :SEQ
OUTPUT :VAL
END

TO PUT :NUM
MAKE "SEQ LPUT :NUM :SEQ
END
```

Beware of subtraction and division; they are not quite what you would expect. For example, entering 12, then 24, then '/' will result in 2 being printed, rather than 0.5. You can add further operations by adding lines to R.POLISH. One useful addition is an operation which merely deletes the last number, in case you enter a wrong number by mistake. Another useful operation is that of swapping the last two items around.

4.7.2 Beautiful Printing, Part 2

The set of procedures described below are designed to print the definition of a procedure, on the screen, in a way similar to the one used in this book. In particular, the printout avoids having any words split by overlapping the right-hand edge of the Apple II screen. For example, rather than seeing a procedure printed on the Apple's 40-character wide screen somewhat like this:

```
TO RUBBISH
 PRINT [THIS IS AN EXAMPLE OF A LIST WIT
H TEN ELEMENTS]
END
```

(the word WITH looks as though it has been split into WIT and H because it overlaps the right-hand edge of the screen), it would be more attractive and less confusing to see

```
THE TEXT OF RUBBISH IS
TO RUBBISH
   PRINT [ THIS IS AN EXAMPLE OF A LIST
        WITH TEN ELEMENTS ]
END
```

It is only possible to do this if the definition of a procedure is available in a form that other procedures can use.
Fortunately, the definition of the procedure is acessible in the
form of a list of lists by using the Terrapin LOGO procedure
TEXT. It expects one input, a word naming a procedure. It outputs
a list of lists, one list per line. The first list holds the inputs
from the title line, or is empty if there are no inputs for the
named procedure. An example: if the procedure JUNK is defined
as

```
TO JUNK :A :B
REPEAT :A [PRINT :B]
END
```

then TEXT "JUNK will output

```
[[:A :B] [REPEAT :A [PRINT :B]]]
```

To use the LOGO procedures below, give the command NICE with
one input, a word naming the procedure whose definition is to be
printed. There are no comments about the definitions; treat them
as an exercise in trying to read LOGO programs. The definitions
could be improved a little; try NICE "PLIST to see where.

```
TO NICE :N
PRINT SENTENCE [THE TEXT OF] SENTENCE :N
    "IS
PRINT1 :N
MAKE "N TEXT :N
PRINT FIRST :N
PLLIST BUTFIRST :N
END

TO PLLIST :N
IF :N = [] THEN PRINT "END STOP
PLIST FIRST :N
PLLIST BUTFIRST :N
END

TO PLIST :L
MAKE "COL 2
PRINT1 "'   '
PP :L
PRINT "
END

TO PP :L
IF :L = [] THEN STOP
IF LIST? FIRST :L THEN PP (SENTENCE "'[
    FIRST :L "]') PP BUTFIRST :L STOP
```

```
IF COUNT FIRST :L > 37 - :COL THEN PRINT
    [] PRINT1 "'        ' MAKE "COL 6
PRINT1 FIRST :L
PRINT1 "' '
MAKE "COL :COL + 1 + COUNT FIRST :L
PP BUTFIRST :L
END
```

The COUNT procedure used here is the version which works whether the input is a word or a list.

Chapter 5
Undertaking a project

Aims Being able to define and use new procedures is only one kind of LOGO skill. There are more general ones which can only be learnt by undertaking some larger-scale enterprises. This chapter is mainly devoted to two unretouched project studies. The aim is to show the bad decisions along the way as well as the good.

5.1 GENERALITIES

What is needed when you undertake a major project goes beyond the skills needed to be able to express ideas as procedures. The work of a project often divides into two parts: the planning, and the implementation of the plans. Although some planning must be done first, do not think that all the decision-making must be completed before starting on the job of implementation. This very rarely works out, not least because it is almost impossible to forecast all the snags beforehand. Moreover, few projects are so fully and clearly defined that it is possible to plan them in complete detail; such projects usually turn out to be dull, anyway.

Nevertheless, planning and implementation are very different activities. It is the norm to have many periods of one and many of the other, interleaved. However, **beware** of trying to do both at once. Only a very experienced programmer can appear to do both at once. Even then it is only appearance, he will still be using his experience to implement something whose planning side he had thoroughly explored months or years ago. Unless you have years of experience to call on, it is better to work somewhat in this fashion:

- Having chosen a project, begin by trying to describe what will first give you some real sense of satisfaction. You may well

125

not be satisfied with it by the time you achieve it, but it will have been a milestone.

- Then plan, in as top-down a fashion as you feel at ease with. That is, try to start with general intentions and refine them stage by stage into more specific intentions.

- When you feel that some of the ingredients are sufficiently precisely defined, implement them. You will probably find it necessary to do this before all the planning is complete, in order to reassure yourself that you are still working along reasonable lines. Planning needs confidence; implementation provides it or proves it unjustified.

- Continue with stages of planning and programming until you reach your milestone or find that you cannot. In either case find another milestone and carry on.

Use paper and pencil when planning. You do not have to make elaborate notes, you can probably get away with jotting down terse reminders of important points. Although you may be one of the few who can work reliably by memory alone, it is vastly more annoying to start by supposing this and being proved wrong than it is to work the other way around.

The rest of this chapter is taken up by two sections, each devoted to a project. Each section has various subsections. The idea is to show two realistic examples, as might be done by a person with a reasonable amount of experience. Working from the point of view of a novice might exhaust your interest.

5.2 NESTED POLYGONS

This project arose from the kind of doodles I do absent-mindedly, such as when concentrating on speaking on the telephone. Looking at the doodles afterward, a certain conjecture came to mind. The project was an attempt to gather some evidence to see if it was really plausible.

5.2.1 The Question

Imagine that you have drawn a somewhat irregular hexagon on your telephone pad. An idle thing to do is to join up the midpoints of the sides. The result is a smaller irregular hexagon. Do it again and again. Figure 5.1 shows the outcome of this after a few minutes. The odd thing is that the innermost hexagon looks much more like a regular hexagon than the original one. Perhaps the more you continue, the more like a regular hexagon it gets. On the other hand it may be only a coincidence, perhaps the initial hexagon was a lucky choice. Maybe some initial hexagons do lead to regular ones and others do not, but if so, why, and what makes the difference? Moreover, what about octagons, heptagons, pentagons? What about quadrilaterals – do you get squares or do you get parallelograms or do you get nothing remarkable at all?[1]

The initial idea, therefore, is to devise some LOGO procedures to draw the successively smaller hexagons. This will make it possible to check on a variety of initial hexagons with comparative ease. The first hurdle is to figure out how this can be done.

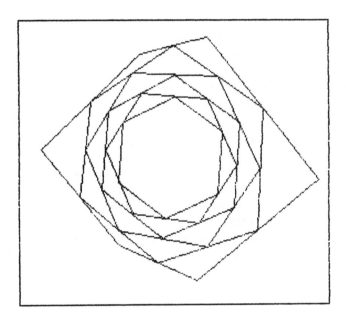

Figure 5.1

1 There is a neat mathematical solution to the problem, based on expressing the co-ordinates as trigonometric polynomials. But suppose that is too much like hard work …

5.2.2 Representing The Hexagon

Experience will teach you that this is one of the most crucial decisions in almost any project. The right decision can make the whole thing easy; the wrong one can lead to high blood pressure and premature philately.

Two possibilities are apparent. The first is to represent the hexagon as a series of FORWARD and RIGHT pairs, as in the RECORD procedure in section 4.6.2.

Advantages   It is easy to produce the actual drawing.

Disadvantages   It is hard to specify the initial list of lists of pairs of numbers, even if the initial hexagon is nearly regular. Also, it is not immediately clear how to get the representation of the nested hexagon from this one.

The other possibility is to represent the hexagon as a list of six elements each giving the co-ordinates of a corner.

Advantages   It is easy to draw the hexagon, using SETXY. It is also easy to specify the initial list – use the RECORD system in chapter 4. It is not too awkward to construct the list that will represent the nested hexagon, either. Given the co-ordinates of two adjacent corners, the co-ordinates of the mid-point can be found by taking the average of the corresponding co-ordinates.

Disadvantages   No major ones (yet).

Therefore, use the second one.

It helps further deliberations if you have a real example to work on. Rather than deal with negative numbers, take a hexagon that lies entirely within the top right quadrant of the screen, say

[[10 30] [30 20] [80 10] [120 80] [50 110] [10 50]]

The procedure PLAYBACK defined in section 6.2 of chapter 4 could be used to draw the hexagon represented by this. It is not ideal – try it, e.g.

```
MAKE "HEX [[10 30] [30 20] [80 10] [120
      80] [50 110] [10 50]]
PLAYBACK :HEX
```

draws figure 5.2. There are two snags. The line from the turtle's starting position to the first corner should not be there. Also, the last side is missing. All would be well if the turtle had started at the last corner. This suggests a simple amendment – make PLAYBACK a subprocedure of one that puts the turtle at the last corner first, and then invokes it. So,

```
TO PLOT :LL
PENUP
SETXY (ITEM 1 LAST :LL ) (ITEM 2 LAST
      :LL )
PENDOWN
PLAYBACK :LL
END
```

This works.

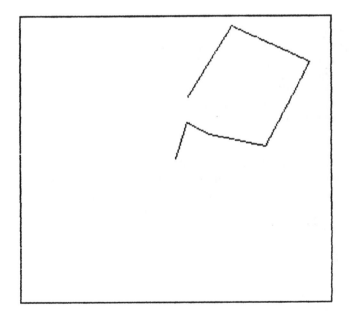

Figure 5.2

5.2.3 Producing The Nested Hexagon

Given one hexagon, the nested one has its corners at the mid-points of the sides. Suppose a side runs from corner [x1 y1] to corner [x2 y2]. The midpoint will have X co-ordinate (x1+x2)/2 and Y co-ordinate (y1+y2)/2. It seems sensible to define a procedure MIDPT which will be given two points (as two-element lists) as inputs, and will output the two-element list for the midpoint:

```
TO MIDPT :PT1 :PT2
OUTPUT LIST ((ITEM 1 :PT1 ) + (ITEM
     1 :PT2 ))/2 ((ITEM 2 :PT1 ) + (
     ITEM 2 :PT2 ))/2
END
```

Try this to make sure that it does the right thing, before carrying on.

It must now be straightforward to define a procedure that, given the representation of a hexagon, outputs the representation of the nested hexagon. For example:

```
TO NEST :LL
OUTPUT (LIST MIDPT ITEM 1 :LL ITEM 2 :LL
     MIDPT ITEM 2 :LL ITEM 3 :LL
     MIDPT ITEM 3 :LL ITEM 4 :LL
     MIDPT ITEM 4 :LL ITEM 5 :LL
     MIDPT ITEM 5 :LL ITEM 6 :LL
     MIDPT ITEM 6 :LL ITEM 1 :LL )
END
```

This one-line procedure is a big mouthful. If you mistyped it the mistake would be hard to find. Moreover, if you were to call the input LISTOFLISTS rather than LL, you would find that Terrapin LOGO would not accept it because the line was too long. The limit is 256 characters. However, NEST works: try

PRINT NEST :HEX

You should be able to predict that it prints

[[20 25] [55 15] [100 45] [85 95] [30 80] [10 40]]

by looking at the value of HEX.

Principle

In general, whenever you create a procedure, try it at once. Don't store up troubles for later.

5.2.4 Trying It Out

You now have the ingredients to start experimenting, namely PLOT
and NEST. You might be tempted to launch into

```
CS
PLOT :HEX
REPEAT 10 [MAKE "HEX NEST :HEX PLOT
     :HEX]
```

but wait. Doing this, you would lose the original value of HEX.
Keep a copy of it first:

```
MAKE "ORIG.HEX :HEX
```

Then the sequence of commands above will produce figure 5.3.
Now you can spend a little time investigating the original conjecture.

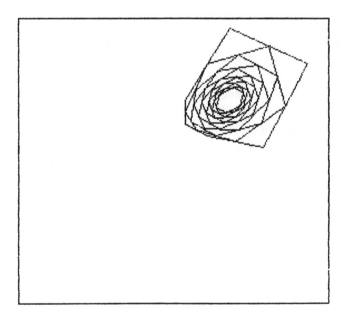

Figure 5.3

5.2.5 Problems And Doubts

If you have now tried nesting hexagons several times, starting from various initial hexagons, you might think that the original conjecture is fractionally more plausible than it seemed earlier. However, the innermost hexagon is eventually too small to judge by eye for regularity.

At this point, another doubt might assail you. If you want to move on to looking at heptagons (seven-sided figures) you need a new version of NEST; you need a new one every time you want to move on to another number of sides. This would be nearly acceptable if NEST weren't so easy to mistype.

Principle

A warning sign in any project is that one or more of the procedures seems to be getting out of hand.

Perhaps it is possible to define a recursive version of NEST, so that it will work however many sides there are. The algorithm, relying on past experience, might go like this:

(a)   If there is only one corner output the empty list.

(b)   Form the midpoint of the first two corners. Join this onto the list of midpoints formed by starting with the BUTFIRST of the original list, and then output the result.

This is incomplete. If it is applied to a list of six corners it generates a list of five midpoints. The missing one is the one lying between the last corner and the first one.

There are at least two possible cures. One is to create a variable which holds the first corner, and then use the value of it in a new step (a):

(a)   If there is only one corner in the list, output the list whose sole element is the midpoint between it and the corner whose position is given by the variable.

Another solution is to change the representation of the polygon slightly. Instead of having N elements,

[corner1 corner2 .. cornerN]

let it have N+1:

    [corner1 corner2 .. cornerN corner1]

This lets you generate all the N midpoints by a straight forward recursion, as outlined above. To construct the representation of the nested polygon all that is needed is to glue a copy of the first midpoint onto the end of the list of midpoints.

5.2.6 The New Nest Procedure

The two solutions are almost equally good. The second one, a changed representation, will be adopted for what follows. It is marginally neater, though neither solution necessitates changes to PLOT.

Principle

> When in genuine doubt, make a random choice – at least it's progress.

NEST becomes:

```
TO NEST :LL
MAKE "LL MIDPTLIST :LL
OUTPUT LPUT (FIRST :LL ) :LL
END

TO MIDPTLIST :LL
IF (COUNT :LL ) = 1 THEN OUTPUT []
OUTPUT FPUT (MIDPT ITEM 1 :LL ITEM 2
      :LL ) (MIDPTLIST BUTFIRST :LL )
END
```

This uses COUNT as defined in section 4.5.4. An interesting detail is the use of LL as though it were a normal variable rather than an input, in the first line of NEST. It was explained in chapter 3 that inputs are variables; the only point to remember is that LL supersedes any other variable of the same name while NEST is being run.

Remember to amend the value of HEX (and ORIG.HEX):

```
MAKE "HEX LPUT (FIRST :HEX ) :HEX
```

5.2.7 **Fault Tracing**

It is timely to discuss how to set about tracking down faults in procedures, using a specific example. Suppose that you have just copied MIDPTLIST into your LOGO system, but you carelessly omitted the BUTFIRST in the last line. When you use NEST, nothing happens, not even a prompt to show that it has finished. The best thing to do is to type CTRL-G to terminate whatever is happening, with extreme prejudice. Thereafter, begin by looking at the definitions of NEST and MIDPTLIST. If the problem doesn't catch your eye one recourse is to include some extra commands in each definition. You could insert

    CHECK "LL

at the start of each definition; CHECK was defined in section 4.5.2. Running NEST again, you should see that LL only changed value once, and thereafter never changed. This might alert you to the problem; MIDPTLIST ought to be invoking itself recursively with successively shorter input lists each time.

The ultimate recourse is to use the Terrapin LOGO procedure TRACE. From the time it is obeyed until the procedure NOTRACE is obeyed, LOGO will print out any line of procedure definition that it is just about to obey. Moreover, LOGO will wait for you to type any character, other than CTRL-G or CTRL-Z, before obeying it. If you type CTRL-G, LOGO will abort every procedure in progress and return to waiting for your next command, as usual. If you type CTRL-Z, LOGO will also wait for commands from you, but the procedures in progress will not have been aborted, merely suspended. (The procedure PAUSE also achieves this effect; PAUSE is to CTRL-Z as TOPLEVEL is to CTRL-G.) You can then give commands to find out such details as the current values of variables. When you want LOGO to resume the suspended procedures, use the command CONTINUE (or CO for short). Using CTRL-Z for fault finding is sometimes not very useful, because it can be hard to find out how far LOGO has got before you typed the CTRL-Z. PAUSE is more useful; you can put it in a known place.

All these fault finding aids may help you. It is hard to give more advice; everyone develops their own style of setting about the hunt, and everyone gets plenty of opportunities to develop it! Just bear these points in mind:

- Be patient.

- Be systematic.

- 99% of all faults are simple ones and have a single cause.

- Test each of your procedures in turn, using various test cases for inputs: 'likely' values, 'unlikely' values and special cases such as the empty list or the empty word.

- Work from the bottom up; test those procedures first which depend least on other procedures. This spares you a lot of trouble if it turns out that there is more than one fault to be found.

- KEEP NOTES!

5.2.8 More About Nested Polygons

Both NEST and PLOT now cope with a polygon of any number of sides. There still remains the problem of what to do when the innermost nested polygon becomes too small to judge properly. One proposal is to switch from drawing the polygon to printing out the lengths of the sides. Presumably more regular polygons have sides which are more nearly equal:

```
TO PRINTSIDES :LL
IF (COUNT :LL ) = 1 THEN STOP
PRINT PYTHAG (ITEM 1 :LL ) (ITEM 2
     :LL )
PRINTSIDES BUTFIRST :LL
END

TO PYTHAG :PT1 :PT2
OUTPUT SQRT (SQR (ITEM 1 :PT1 ) −
     (ITEM 1 :PT2 )) + (SQR (ITEM
     2 :PT1 ) −(ITEM 2 :PT2 ))
END

TO SQR :N
OUTPUT :N * :N
END
```

It turns out, however, that this idea is not very good. The side lengths get so small that it is tricky to compare them; it is hard to assess whether they are getting 'more equal' with successive nestings.

What is really needed is a new idea - or to give up on the whole problem.

Principle

When all else fails, indulge in wishful or fantastic speculations.

If you want to try your hand at thinking of a solution to this problem, then **do** **not** **look** **at** **the** **next** **page** **yet.** Put the book down and think about it for a little while.

The problem of minute nested polygons would not be so bad if you had a powerful magnifying glass for peering at the screen. This suggests an idea: why not magnify the polygon every so often? How often? Answer: when you feel it necessary. How can you magnify a polygon? Simply multiply every co-ordinate by some chosen scaling-up factor. What factor? Rather than indulging in an orgy of calculation, why not just pick one and see? You can always erase the screen and try another if your choice is bad.

First, consider how to rescale one single point:

```
TO RESCALE :PT :SCALE
OUTPUT LIST :SCALE * (ITEM 1 :PT )
     :SCALE * (ITEM 2 :PT )
END
```

To magnify the whole polygon just RESCALE each corner in turn:

```
TO MAGNIFY :LL :SCALE
IF :LL = [] THEN STOP
OUTPUT FPUT (RESCALE FIRST :LL :SCALE )
     (MAGNIFY BUTFIRST :LL :SCALE )
END
```

To try this, the first thing is to recover the original hexagon – the test case – and to clear the screen:

```
CS
MAKE "HEX :ORIG.HEX
```

Then do some nesting:

```
REPEAT 10 [MAKE "HEX NEST :HEX PLOT :HEX]
```

Then magnify the final one a bit:

```
MAKE "HEX MAGNIFY :HEX 6
```

Now the magnified hexagon may not fit the screen. You can print it and check that no co-ordinate is outside the area of the screen. On the other hand you could just clear the screen and PLOT it. If it is too small or big, just use MAGNIFY again with a suitable scaling factor.

5.2.9 The Next Snag

The trick of magnification lets you continue the nesting process for a while. However, you will find that magnification tends to make the polygon drift off to the edge of the screen. (For the technically minded: magnification moves the centre of area of the polygon further from the centre of the screen, so you would expect this.) The remedy is clear: move the magnified polygon across a bit. This means adding a chosen number to every X co-ordinate, and another chosen number to every Y co-ordinate. A tidy way to specify the two numbers is as a list with two elements, e.g. [50 30] meaning 'add 50 to the X co-ordinates, add 30 to the Y co-ordinates'. To adjust one corner is easy:

```
TO ADJUST :PT :AMOUNT
OUTPUT LIST (ITEM 1 :PT ) + (ITEM 1
     :AMOUNT ) (ITEM 2 :PT ) + (ITEM
     2 :AMOUNT )
END
```

Shifting the whole polygon is almost as easy:

```
TO SHIFT :LL :AMOUNT
IF :LL = [] THEN STOP
OUTPUT FPUT (ADJUST FIRST :LL :AMOUNT )
     (SHIFT BUTFIRST :LL :AMOUNT )
END
```

To use it:

```
MAKE "HEX SHIFT :HEX [-50 -60]
```

You now have a toolkit which allows you to pursue the original conjecture as far as you want.

PLOT   This draws a polygon on the screen.

NEST   This constructs the list of lists representing the next nested polygon.

MAGNIFY This is used whenever the polygon gets too small.

SHIFT   This is used whenever the polygon drifts too far from the middle of the screen.

EXERCISES

(1)   Investigate the conjecture. If it's false, can you modify it to fit the facts from the investigation?

(2)   Would you come to a different conclusion if you formed nested polygons according to a different rule? For instance, instead of midpoints use one of the points of trisection of each side.

(3)   A very interesting variation is to form the nested polygon by joining the midpoints of diagonals instead of sides. To start with, use the diagonals which link each corner to the one two round from it.

(4)   Have you tried using really irregular polygons, such as non-convex ones (that is, having one or more inward bulges)?

5.3 DIFFERENT NUMBER BASES

This project was originally mentioned in a paper[1] describing a study of how LOGO might be used in a school mathematics classroom. The work was funded by the Social Science Research Council of Great Britain.

Numbers are conventionally written 'in base 10'. This means that the group of digits

754

is the conventional way of writing the number

7*100 + 5*10 + 4*1

The multipliers, from right to left, are 1, 10 and 100: successive powers of 10. If you were told that 754 was really meant to be read 'in base 8' here, the number in question would have been

7*64 + 5*8 +4*1

which is 448 + 40 + 4 or 492 in the customary 'base 10' notation. The multipliers here, from right to left, are 1, 8 and 64: successive powers of eight. In base 8 numbers, the digits '8' and '9' are not used. The reason is that if they were, there would be at least two different ways of expressing most numbers, for

1 'Teaching Mathematics through Programming in the Classroom', by J.A.M.Howe, P.M.Ross, K.Johnson and R.Inglis, **Computers and Education**, vol. 6, 1982

example, the number written '91' would be

    9*8 + 1

which is the same as

    (8 + 1)*8 + 1

which is

    1*64 + 1*8 + 1

which can be written in base 8 as '111'. Similarly, when numbers are written in base 2 notation, the only digits are '0' and '1'. It is important to realise that when dealing with numbers in unconventional bases, it is only the **representation** of the numbers, as marks on paper or syllables in speech, that is different. The number written as '43' in base 8 is exactly the same number denoted by '35' in base 10, or by '50' in base 7, or by '100011' in base 2.

The aim of this project is to devise a set of LOGO procedures for experimenting with numbers written in unconventional bases. The motive is pure curiosity.

5.3.1 First Thoughts

The first need that comes to mind is for a means of converting a number from one base to another. Take an example: how is '91' in base 10 to be written in base 8? It is bigger than 64 and less than 512 (=64*8), so the leftmost digit in the base 8 representation will be standing for the number of 64s involved. Now

    91 = 1*64 + 27

so the leftmost digit will be one. The remainder, 27, is

    27 = 3*8 + 3

so

    91 = 1*64 + 3*8 + 3*1

and therefore '91' is written as '133' in base 8. It should be possible to formalise this somehow, though it may look confusing at the moment.

In fact, the method looks sufficiently confusing to make one think twice. The problem is to determine what the digits are when

91 is rewritten in base 8. Suppose they are A, B and C. Then

$$91 = A*64 + B*8 + C*1$$

The right-hand side of this is C plus some multiple of 8, because A*64 + B*8 is a sum of multiples of 8. This means that C is just the remainder when 91 is divided by 8 – and there is a LOGO procedure REMAINDER to work this out in any general case. Since 91 = 11*8 + 3, C must be 3. Moreover,

$$11*8 = A*64 + B*8$$

so

$$11 = A*8 + B$$

This means that 'AB' is the representation of 11 in base 8. By the same process, B is 3 and A is 1.

Formalise this. Instead of working with 91, consider how to do it for any number – call the number N. The final digit of the representation of N in base 8 is the remainder when N is divided by 8. Unfortunately this is, literally, the last digit to be written down. As the example above suggests, the digits that come earlier are those which form the representation, in base 8, of the integer quotient on N divided by 8. There is a LOGO procedure QUOTIENT to work this out. There is also one easy point to note: it is only when N is more than 7 that you need to consider quotients at all.

A restatement of all this, closer to LOGO, is

(a)   If N is more than 7, write the base 8 representation of the integer quotient of N divided by 8.

(b)   Write the remainder of dividing N by 8.

This turns directly into LOGO:

```
TO BASE8 :N
IF :N > 7 THEN BASE8 QUOTIENT :N 8
PRINT1 REMAINDER :N 8
END
```

PRINT1 is used, rather than PRINT, so that the digits all appear on the same line. It is also easy to generalise BASE8 so that it works for other bases. Let the base be given as the value of a variable called BASE. A suitable generalisation might be:

```
TO CONVERT :N
IF :N > (:BASE - 1 ) THEN CONVERT
    QUOTIENT :N :BASE
PRINT1 REMAINDER :N :BASE
END
```

Test this.

```
MAKE "BASE 2
CONVERT 30
```

prints 11110. However, there is room for improvement:

```
MAKE "BASE 8
CONVERT 13.216
```

prints 15.

5.3.2 Difficulties

There are faults. In particular,

- It gets negative numbers wrong.

- It would be more useful if it could OUTPUT something instead of PRINTing.

- If the base is larger than 10, the number it prints is very odd because, for instance, it will treat a remainder of 10 as though it were a single digit.

- It ignores anything after a decimal point in the input. This is because both QUOTIENT and REMAINDER round their inputs to be integers.

Each of these is understandable but annoying. The immediate question is the order in which to try tackling them. It is wise to leave the first one till last, for this reason:

Principle

When a number of difficulties compete equally for your attention, try the most all-embracing or most elaborate one first. If you solve it, some of the others may disappear. If you cannot (yet) solve it, move on to the next worst.

Applying this is hard: it is only your opinion as to which is the worst. In this case the question of decimals looks very intractable; the earlier discussion never got round to them at all. The best thing to do is to ignore it, by deciding that CONVERT will only be used with integers.

Principle

If a problem looks too nasty, change the rules.

It is amazing how few people make conscious use of this, although it is a valuable and much-applied principle in every branch of mathematics. When you have made enough progress with the amended problem, you may begin to see how to tackle the original.

The second and third deficiencies of CONVERT go hand in hand. One answer to the problem of representing outsize digits is commonly used in computer science, namely to use letters as extra digits. The sixteen possible digits in base 16 – a digit being defined as something that is acceptable as a 'place value' in the written form of a number – are conventionally denoted by '0',...'9', 'A',...'F'. But there are only 26 letters (most Apples do not have lower case) and so there is still a problem if the base is bigger than 36. The crux of the trouble is that it seems necessary to use a single symbol for a single digit. If you were to use a pair of symbols, it would always be possible for two pairs to appear side by side in the written form, and so cause confusion. To illustrate this: imagine you are a Venusian on the point of inventing written forms of numbers. You ponder using ' ' for the Earthling '1', and ' ' for the Earthling '2'. It is a bad choice – would the Venusian ' ' be the Earthling '111', or '12', or '21'?

The way forward is to ignore that problem. Now look at the second deficiency, wanting to make CONVERT output instead of print. What sort of thing can any procedure output? A word, number or list. A list looks best: why not make CONVERT output a list of digits, for instance, [9 1] to represent 91 in base 10? In fact why not include the base in the list – why not decide that 91 will be represented as [9 1 [10]]? The base is itself within a list, to avoid thinking of it as another digit.

The more you consider this, the better it looks. The list would be easy to read when PRINTed, since PRINT omits the outermost brackets. The number '-91' can be represented as [-9 1 [10]]. Also, the problem of representing outsized digits goes away! Now that there is a space between each digit when a number is printed, it is perfectly satisfactory to use two or more symbols together to represent one single digit. For example the number 22, when represented in base 12, would be the list [1 10 [12]]. This is unambiguous.

This gives you a good example of how the two general principles stated earlier can work out advantageously in practice. The final deficiency of CONVERT has also been resolved by adopting the list notation. To CONVERT a negative number, convert the positive number and glue a minus sign onto the front of the result.

5.3.3 Redesigning The Procedure

Things have now moved from planning to implementation. There are three ingredients, not necessarily in this order:

- Constructing the list of digits.

- Attaching the information about the base to the end of the list.

- Worrying about whether the number is negative or positive. This must be the first step.

There ought to be a sub-procedure for generating the unadorned list of digits. This procedure will only ever have a positive input.

The algorithm for this sub-procedure resembles the previous one for CONVERT:

(a)   If the input, :N, is more than :BASE − 1 then output the list formed by

    (i)   getting the digit list of QUOTIENT :N :BASE

    (ii)   attaching REMAINDER :N :BASE to the end of this list, by using LPUT

(b)   Otherwise just output the list whose sole element is :N.

In LOGO this is:

```
TO DIGIT.LIST :N
TEST :N > (:BASE − 1 )
IFTRUE OUTPUT LPUT (REMAINDER :N :BASE )
     (DIGIT.LIST QUOTIENT :N :BASE )
IFFALSE OUTPUT (LIST :N )
END
```

The new CONVERT procedure will use this. The plan is:

(a)   If the input is negative, then change the sign and FPUT a
       minus sign onto the list formed by glueing the details of
       the base onto the end of the result of DIGIT.LIST.

(b)   Otherwise just glue the details of the base onto the end
       of the result of DIGIT.LIST.

Thus

```
TO CONVERT :N
TEST :N < 0
IFTRUE OUTPUT FPUT "- LPUT (LIST :BASE )
     DIGIT.LIST (-:N )
IFFALSE OUTPUT LPUT (LIST :BASE )
     DIGIT.LIST :N
END
```

Test this with various bases.

There is one base other than 10 that is widely used, though
you may not immediately think of it as such. It is base 1000. It is
used when the number 19723 is written as '19,723'.

5.3.4 Recovering The Base 10 Form

It would be useful to be able to recover the conventional form of
a number – the base 10 form. The alternatives are to devise a
method for this from scratch, or to devise a method which is the
inverse of the one used in defining DIGIT.LIST.

Take the former. An example: 95 is [1 3 7 [8]]. The first
thing to do with the list is to prune off the final element, using
LAST and BUTLAST, to get hold of the digit list and the base
separately. The base is the FIRST of the LAST, the digit list is
the BUTLAST, [1 3 7]. There are two ways to look at this. One is
that it is 1*64 + whatever [3 7] represents in base 8. This looks
difficult; why 64 rather than 8 or 512? The other way is to think
of it as 8 times whatever [1 3] represents, + 7. This way is
better, it has a more natural correspondence with ideas of recursion in LOGO. It is akin to observing that

    1*64 + 3*8 + 7

is the same as

    (((1)*8 + 3)*8 + 7)

though it is not important to grasp this. Here is a LOGO procedure to turn a digit list back into a number; the base is
assumed to be given as the value of a variable BB:

```
TO RECOVER :DL
IF :DL = [] THEN OUTPUT 0
OUTPUT (:BB * RECOVER BUTLAST :DL )
    + (LAST :DL )
END
```

This will be a sub-procedure of the main one, say DEC. The
steps in DEC will be:

(a)   Check if there is a minus sign at the start of the input
list. If so, remove it and then output the negative of the
number obtained by doing the following steps.

(b)   Prune off the last element, the base information, and set
a variable called BB to be the base.

(c)   Use RECOVER to get the value.

In LOGO this is

```
TO DEC :L
IF "- = FIRST :L THEN OUTPUT (- DEC
    BUTFIRST :L )
MAKE "BB FIRST LAST :L
OUTPUT RECOVER BUTLAST :L
END
```

if you are doubtful of the translation from algorithm to LOGO, then
work through, on paper, what happens during the command

```
PRINT DEC [- 1 3 7 [8]]
```

Now the armoury for investigating numbers in different bases
consists of CONVERT and DEC. There are two extensions:

- It would be useful if CONVERT also accepted a list as input,
so that it could convert a number not in base 10 to yet
another base.

- It would be useful to have procedures to do simple arithmetic
using the list forms of numbers.

Both of these are easy.

5.3.5 Improving CONVERT And DEC

The improvement to CONVERT consists of checking whether the input is a list. It it is, just use DEC to turn it into a base 10 number first:

```
TO CONVERT :N
IF LIST? :N THEN MAKE "N DEC :N
etc. etc.
END
```

The improvement to DEC consists of checking whether the input is a number. If it is just output it:

```
TO DEC :L
IF NUMBER? :L THEN OUTPUT :L
etc. etc.
END
```

5.3.6 Arithmetic In Any Base

About the hardest task in devising arithmetic procedures is choosing names for them. Use ADD, SUBTRACT, MULTIPLY and DIVIDE. The procedure ADD is

```
TO ADD :N1 :N2
OUTPUT CONVERT ((DEC :N1 ) + (DEC :N2 ))
END
```

and the others are similarly defined. Here is a sample session of using the procedures:

```
?MAKE "BASE 8
?MAKE "X CONVERT 15
?MAKE "Y CONVERT 17
?PRINT :X
1 7 [8]
?PRINT :Y
2 1 [8]
?MAKE "BASE 16
?PRINT CONVERT 15*17
15 15 [16]
?PRINT CONVERT (MULTIPLY :X :Y )
15 15 [16]
?PRINT CONVERT :X
15 [16]
```

```
?PRINT CONVERT :Y
1 1 [16]
?PRINT DEC MULTIPLY :X :Y
255
?MAKE BASE 2
?PRINT CONVERT 255
1 1 1 1 1 1 1 1 [2]
```

and so on. Observations such as the fact that [15 [16]] multiplied by [1 1 [16]] is [15 15 [16]] will help to give you a feel for simple arithmetic in bases other than 10.

EXERCISES

(5)   Is it sensible for the base to be negative, using the current procedure definitions? If not, can they be suitably modified?   Is the idea of a negative base reasonable?

(6)   Can you now extend the work to cover numbers with decimal parts?   (Hint: 3.74 is 374/100)

(7)   Is the idea of a non-integer base reasonable? The existing procedures are not adequate for investigating this.

5.4 A FINAL PROJECT

Various general principles were mentioned in this chapter. Keep them in mind when you embark on any of the projects outlined in chapter 7. Other useful general maxims will strike you as you get more experienced. The only one you ought to stick to without exception is

KEEP NOTES!

There is the basis of another project: how was the diagram produced?

Chapter 6
Ideas and where they might come from

"Is that you, Rabbit?" said Pooh.
"Let's suppose it isn't," said Rabbit, "and
see what happens."

(The House at Pooh Corner, A.A.Milne)

Aims In most projects there comes a point at which you find yourself stuck, if only temporarily. This chapter offers a few thoughts and strategies which may help you when you are in a mess.

6.1 PICKING A PROJECT

"Project?", many people say to themselves, "well .. um .. I can't think of one." There is a widespread fancy that having sufficient originality of mind to think up a worthwhile project and carry it through, is (a) rare, (b) a gift rather than an acquisition, (c) a personal characteristic which is somehow independent of experience and knowledge. It is not so. Confidence is a major factor in determining success. While success also creates confidence, there are other sources as well.

The best way to pick a project is to select something which has caught your interest. Your interest gets you started, and keeps you going on those frequent occasions when your expertise temporarily fails you. The object of the interest does not have to be part of the world of LOGO. The initial thought can be very woolly:

- write procedures to generate chunks of English text

- investigate ways of tiling a floor

149

- devise mazes

- experiment with abstract patterns

- play chess

and may turn out to be impossible.

The initial idea does not have to be specific, or sharply defined. If it is not, you can take for a project the task of seeing to what extent the initial idea is practicable. Bear in mind that trying but failing to do the project is just as worthwhile as succeeding. In fact, it is usually more worthwhile, since you will probably have done more investigating.

Do not set your sights too low. In particular, do not reject a project idea on the grounds that you cannot immediately see how to turn the details into LOGO. On the other hand, do not set your sights too high. A useful guard against this is to measure how much description the idea needs. Suppose you think, "I'll get LOGO to play me at chess." As you probably know, playing chess in anything other than a mindless way demands some experience and some ability to look forward. Even writing down the fundamental rules takes a while to do. All this would have to be captured somehow within LOGO procedures, not necessarily explicitly but at least in such a manner that a person who knew LOGO but no chess could learn quite a lot about the game by reading the procedure definitions. Looked at this way, the task is too daunting. It would be possible to narrow the scope, of course. You could make your Apple II into a chessboard, merely recording and displaying the moves of two human players on the screen. Or you could use LOGO as a simple tool to show you how many times each square is attacked; this is useful if you are a devotee of one- and two-move chess problems, or a player of postal chess. Unlike chess, the instructions for tic-tac-toe are very short and a foolproof strategy is easy to explain. A project concerned with playing that game would therefore seem to have a good chance of success, even though you cannot at once envisage the details.

Another fruitful source of project ideas lies in following up possibilities that have occurred to you in earlier work (so keep notes of them). For instance, the Apple II comes equipped with two 'paddles', each having a rotatable knob and a button. Terrapin LOGO provides the means to use them. The procedure PADDLE takes one input, a number between 0 and 3 (the Apple II can accomodate four paddles though only two are provided), and outputs a number between 0 and 255 that depends on how far the

knob on the relevant paddle has been turned. The procedure
PADDLEBUTTON takes a similar input, and outputs TRUE if the
appropriate button is being pressed at the time, or FALSE otherwise. Therefore, you have a means of controlling something. What?
With two paddles you can control two quantities (at least). It may
have struck you, when working through chapter 3, that it would be
nice to have a simple sketching system that is easier to use than
typing in turtle commands. The combination of the ingredients of
paddles, the turtle and the thought about sketching suggests an
idea, namely using SETXY to move the turtle around according to
the rotation of the two knobs.

6.2 EVALUATING IDEAS

When trying to pick a project, or when tackling some part of one,
you are sometimes faced with the job of assessing an idea before
launching into it. The assessment is purely to decide whether the
idea merits the effort of some exploration.

If you do this, it is likely that you are neutral about the idea
in question. If you were emotionally attached to the idea you
would just plunge in. If it did not appeal to you, you might reject
it out of hand. It is surprising, however, how productive a few
moments of consideration can be. There are almost no guidelines
for you; this is another of those matters which depend heavily on
temperament and experience. About the only reliable rules are to
leave questions of programmability until last – LOGO is meant to
be very flexible – and to look into the question of what resources
are required.

As an illustration, consider this question: can LOGO be used
to construct some useful word-processing tools? On the positive
side: it is possible to print words almost anywhere on the screen,
it is easy to determine the length of words, the technical manual
explains how to get things printed on paper, and so on. On the
negative side: with LOGO there is not much free space for the
text itself (how can you check?), a reasonable quality printer is
needed, the Apple II does not readily cope with lower case. The
balance depends on you priorities. If you spend a lot of time
constructing notices using transfer lettering, where the letters are
of various widths, then you can make up a LOGO toolkit containing
all the relevant details to help you lay out the letters on paper.

6.3 LOOKING FOR IDEAS

There are various useful strategies that help in the hunt for ideas.
Generalisation and specialisation are two common ones, and there

are various ways they can be applied. The example of simple shape recording, in section 4.6.2, could be generalised to include the possibility of recording whether the turtle's pen was down or up, and what colour it was, as well as the turtle's position. This would make it possible to record and replay much more sophisticated shapes. The same example could be generalised in another direction entirely, towards simple command recording. A command recording system could be used either to allow you to replay recent commands, or (using DEFINE) to allow you to define a procedure and have the commands obeyed while defining.

Generalisation depends on being able to answer the question "what am I really trying to do here?", in detail. Traditional wisdom says that the thing to do is to write down all your assumptions and aims about the matter in hand, and then pick over the list in a systematic way. If you can do that, you do not need help. The only useful recommendation for you if you cannot specify your assumptions, is to turn over the goals in your mind and pick on the bits that annoy you. Indulge in wishful thinking: ask yourself "wouldn't it be nice if..." and "what would happen if ...". For instance: wouldn't it be nice if LOGO did arithmetic to an accuracy of some large number of significant digits? This is a project discussed further in chapter 7.

Specialisation tends to be easier than generalisation, because it happens more naturally. It arises when you find some goal too hard and you have to cut down your ambition a bit. There have been several examples earlier in this book, such as the limitation of the number bases project to integers only in section 6.3.2. As another simple case: think about defining some LOGO procedures that accept a date as input, and output the day of the week on which it fell, or will fall. It is messy, especially if you want it to work for years before 1752 when the calendar was reformed. Start by working only in the current year. If that is too much, start by working only in the current month of the current year.

Another useful strategy goes by the quaint name of 'defocussing'. The idea is to examine something well known and understood, but consciously to ignore certain aspects of it. It is very much akin to specialisation, but you start with something familiar. This was applied in chapter 2 to the REPEAT command, to see it as a command that contained another command. As another example, look at the procedure CHAR mentioned in section 4.5.4. It is normally used in conjunction with ASCII; ASCII expects a single character word as input, and outputs the number associated with it by international conventions, and CHAR does the reverse. However, CHAR is just a procedure which takes a number as input, and outputs a character. CHAR 65 outputs A, and CHAR

32 ouputs a word consisting of a single space, but there are many more possible numbers to input than there are characters to output. If you investigate, you will make some useful discoveries, such as the fact that CHAR 7 outputs a character which, when PRINTed, causes the Apple II to bleep briefly. In particular, the only effect of

```
PRINT1 CHAR 7
```

is to cause the bleep, and so the command can be used when it is necessary for a procedure to attract your attention.

Perhaps the most useful strategy is analogy. It lets you import ideas, if not solutions, from other domains familiar to you. There are dangers, as you can easily stretch an analogy too far, but it is also the main aid to imagination. Consider the Apple's paddles again. The sketchpad system suggested earlier has a bad drawback; it is hard to control the paddles accurately in order to draw straight lines or smooth curves. A better sketchpad system can be conceived by analogy with a radar screen. Imagine the turtle anchored at a particular spot, moving forward and back a chosen distance along a chosen heading. The distance and heading can be selected by the paddle knobs, so that rotating the knob controlling the heading makes the line repeatedly drawn by the turtle sweep round like a radar beam. If a button is pressed then the turtle leaps to the other end of the beam, and that becomes the new centre of rotation. As a sketchpad system this is much better: all the lines are straight, and it is possible to provide an informative digital readout at the bottom of the screen by using CURSOR. Here are the details; the sketcher is started by the command START:

```
TO START
HOME CS SPLITSCREEN
CURSOR 6 20 PRINT1 "X
CURSOR 20 20 PRINT1 "DISTANCE
CURSOR 6 21 PRINT1 "Y
CURSOR 20 21 PRINT1 "HEADING
SKETCH
END

TO SKETCH
MAKE "X XCOR
MAKE "Y YCOR
SETH 360 * (PADDLE 0 ) / 255
MAKE "D PADDLE 1
CURSOR 8 20
(PRINT1 ROUND :X "'    ' )
CURSOR 29 20
```

```
(PRINT1 ROUND :D "'   ' )
CURSOR 8 21
(PRINT1 ROUND :Y "'   ' )
CURSOR 29 21
(PRINT1 ROUND HEADING "'   ' )
PC 6
FD :D
PU SETXY :X :Y PD
FD :D
PU SETXY :X :Y PD
IF PADDLEBUTTON 0 THEN PC 1 FD :D
SKETCH
END
```

Some points: the beam is drawn by doing FD :D twice, with pen colour 6 (the inverting colour), rather than FD :D and BK :D because sometimes BK :D does not entirely erase all the dots drawn by the FD :D. The only sure way to erase a line is to retrace it in the same direction in which it was drawn. Pen colour 6 is used, rather than the background colour, so that the sketcher does not erase previously drawn parts of the sketch. The captions for the digital readout are printed by START because they only need to be printed once. It is a happy accident that SKETCH is not too fast; if it were then it would be difficult to push the paddlebutton and release it fast enough to prevent LOGO obeying PADDLEBUTTON 0 twice while you still had the button depressed. Try START when the turtle is allowed to wrap.

6.4 WHEN IN A MESS

If you reach the stage of banging your head against the wall, then follow this recipe:

(a)   Rest for a bit.

(b)   Try working on something else, unrelated to the source of your frustration.

(c)   When you are ready, go back and try to crack the nut some other ways.

(d)   If all fails, give up. There is no shame in it; if you find there is, you are probably taking the enterprise too seriously, and you should do step (a) several times in a row.

Such a recipe is as good as any other. None of them are any use unless you have some reasonably-developed self-awareness. Creation, in any area, has several phases: a period of incubation, the 'Eureka' stage when the thoughts hatch, and the stage of thrashing out details. The incubation stage normally takes a while, and proceeds happily while you are doing something else unrelated – so you may as well do something else, such as lie in the bath drinking beer. The 'Eureka' stage is unpredictable, but it need not be sudden or complete. It can equally well appear as a slow increase in certainty that you are on a 'right' track. The thrashing stage is when you actually do the mundane things to make it all work, and is the only phase that an outside observer would recognise as effort.

Chapter 7
Projects

Aims This chapter contains some project suggestions, with thoughts about each. Some have a mathematical bias, others don't. They may look ambitious, but they are all possible.

7.1 PROJECTS WITH CLEAR TARGETS

Projects which have clearly defined objectives are not necessarily any easier than ones with hazy or ridiculously ambitious targets. The first subsection consists of four diagrams, suggesting some drawing projects.

7.1.1 Drawings

The four drawings on the next two pages should give you some ideas. The face was drawn using a sketching procedure of the sort hinted at in chapter 6. The rolling box used nothing more than was in chapter 2. The set of ellipses is the hardest; devising a procedure to draw one is no easy task. The abstract pattern also used the ideas of chapter 2, but the fundamental ingredient was an arc rather than a straight line.

7.1.2 Rotation And Reflection Of Shapes

The result of this project might be a useful tool for introducing this topic to someone unfamiliar with it.

The aim is to produce a set of tools for playing about with shapes, reflecting them in specified lines through the origin and rotating them about the origin. There are various ways this might be done, such as the method used in section 4.6.1. The important feature is that the user of the tools should be able to specify

Figure 7.1

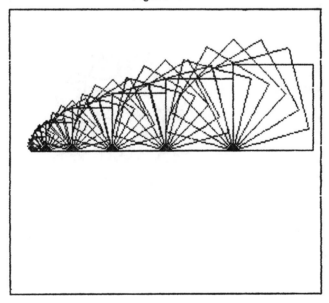

Figure 7.2

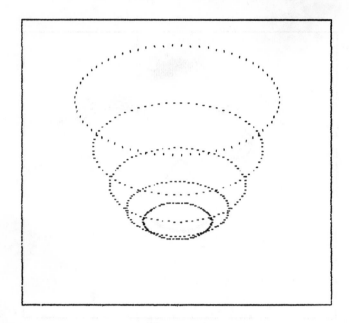

Figure 7.3

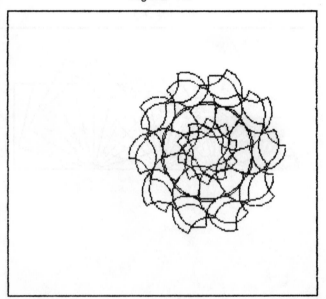

Figure 7.4

some shape to play with, in a straightforward way. Since it is possible to get hold of the definition of a procedure, using TEXT, it would be possible to devise a system that interpreted the definition, putting LEFT for RIGHT when the reflection of a shape was to be drawn. If you try this, it turns out to be rather cumbersome.

The method proposed here, which you need not use, is to require the user to use two new procedures instead of FORWARD and RIGHT, namely AHEAD and TURN:

```
TO AHEAD :DIST
FORWARD :DIST * :SCALE
END

TO TURN :ANGLE
RT :ANGLE * :ASCALE
END
```

The variables SCALE and ASCALE will initially be 1, so that AHEAD and TURN are synonyms for FORWARD and RIGHT. The scale of a shape can be changed simply by altering SCALE and re-running the procedure to draw it. The shape can be drawn as a mirror image, once the turtle is suitably positioned, merely by changing the sign of ASCALE. The value of ASCALE will always be either 1 or −1.

There are two awkward parts to the whole project. One is that shapes defined by the user may not be state-transparent. If they are not, then it will be hard to draw the reflection of a shape in a specified mirror, since the turtle needs to be at the image of the starting place before starting to draw the reflection. A way to get round the problem is to define a procedure SHOW, whose input should be the name of a procedure defining the shape:

```
TO SHOW :SHAPE
MAKE "OLDX XCOR
MAKE "OLDY YCOR
MAKE "OLDH HEADING
REPEAT 1 (LIST :SHAPE )
PU SETXY :OLDX :OLDY PD
SETH :OLDH
END
```

This version only works in a state-transparent way if the shape starts and finishes with the pen down, but you can improve it if you want.

The other tricky part is to figure out how to reflect the turtle's position and heading in a given mirror. The procedures MIRROR and REFLECT, defined below, draw a dotted line representing the mirror along a specified heading through the origin and reflect the turtle in that mirror:

```
TO MIRROR :A
MAKE "OLDX XCOR
```

```
        MAKE "OLDY YCOR
        MAKE "OLDH HEADING
        PU HOME PD
        RT :A
        REPEAT 30 [FD 1 PU FD 3 PD]
        PU HOME PD
        RT 180 + :A
        REPEAT 30 [FD 1 PU FD 3 PD]
        PU SETXY :OLDX :OLDY PD
        SETH :OLDH
        END

        TO REFLECT :A
        MIRROR :A
        MAKE "AA (2 * :A - ATAN XCOR YCOR )
        PU
        SETXY R * SIN :AA R * COS :AA
        SETH (2 * :A - HEADING )
        PD
        END

        TO R
        OUTPUT SQRT (XCOR * XCOR + YCOR * YCOR )
        END
```

This is the bare bones of the set of procedures. It would be an improvement if SHOW also caused the name of the shape it draws to be preserved as the value of some variable, say LAST.DRAWN, so that REFLECT could also draw the reflection of the shape last SHOWn after reversing the sign of ASCALE. Figure 7.5 shows an example of a shape reflected in a 45-degree mirror. A useful extra would be a procedure to rotate the turtle's location about the origin by a given angle, so that the user could play with rotating and reflecting shapes.

7.1.3 Precise Arithmetic

Terrapin LOGO is limited to six significant figures when doing arithmetic. The aim of this project is to extend that considerably, to 30 or more significant figures. While one approach would be to work in base 1000, capitalising on the effort in section 6.3, it is neater and conceptually better to work with lists of digits. For instance, 82371964 could be represented as

    [8 2 3 7 1 9 6 4]

If you wanted to work with decimals as well, it would be better to represent a number such as 82371964.003 as

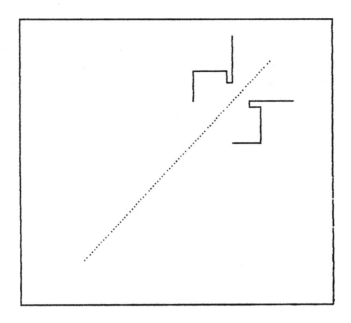

Figure 7.5

[8 2 3 7 1 9 6 4 0 0 3 [-3]]

so that you continue to work essentially with integers, but can adjust the mutiplying power of ten at the end of a calculation. You should start by defining a procedure to add two numbers represented in some such way; this is the easiest of arithmetic operations.

It is awkward to have to enter numbers in a list form. You cannot merely enter them as numbers, because LOGO will treat them as such and give them to your procedure as an approximation correct to six significant figures. The solution is to use READCHARACTER, RC for short, to get hold of the digits and any sign or decimal point one by one. Here is a procedure to get hold of a positive integer. A procedure to read in a positive or negative number, possibly with a decimal part, is rather more complex.

```
TO GETINT :L
MAKE "CHAR RC
PRINT1 :CHAR
IF ALLOF (:CHAR = "' ' ) (:L = [] )
      THEN OUTPUT GETINT :L
IF MEMBER? :CHAR [0 1 2 3 4 5 6 7 8 9]
      THEN OUTPUT GETINT LPUT :CHAR :L
```

```
OUTPUT :L
END
```

This is used by giving it the empty list as input; it glues digits onto the end of its input. The first IF command ensures that any initial spaces are forgotten. The second IF command glues the latest digit onto the end of the story so far, which is handed on as the input to a recursive use of GETINT. If some digits have been collected and the character read by RC is not a digit, then the last line is obeyed, thus ending the collecting of digits. An interesting thought is that the procedure could also be used for collecting words – just use a different list in the MEMBER? check.

Procedures for multiplication and division can be defined essentially by mimicking the way these are done on paper. Terrapin LOGO probably does not have enough space or speed to let you define a high-precision SIN or COS, but you could include the high-precision basic operations with the reverse Polish calculator in section 4.7.1.

7.1.4 Tangrams

This is an ancient chinese puzzle. It consists of seven pieces, as shown in figure 7.6. They are used to try to compose a variety of puzzle shapes, from a simple parallelogram and other regular patterns to elaborate outlines of animals and people. It is possible to write LOGO procedures for playing about with them, although if that is all you want to do it is easier to use cardboard. With quite a lot of work it is possible to devise procedures for analysing an outline, to see if it can be composed of the seven tangrams. The project acquires more point when you start experimenting with sets of pieces of your own choice, rather than the seven in figure 7.6. It is much easier to play about with shapes in LOGO than it is to cut up bits of cardboard every time you want to alter one of the basic shapes somewhat.

The key idea is to represent the outline of a basic shape as a list of lists. Each list in the list contains two numbers, the first being the length of a side and the second being the amount by which to turn right at the end of that side. The list describes the shape in a clockwise direction. When you want to stick two shapes together along an edge, the method for constructing the description of the new shape is suggested by figure 7.7. Copy one shape till you reach the edge where the second is to be attached, then switch to the second shape and copy edges till you meet the edge where the first is to be attached. At the last edge before you switch from first to second shape, you need to

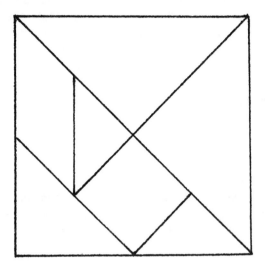

Figure 7.6

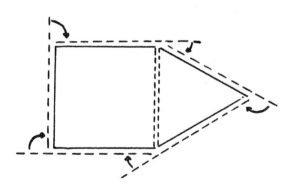

Figure 7.7

adjust the turning angle. A similar adjustment is necessary when stepping from the second to the first.

A neat trick which greatly simplifies the programming is to describe a shape by going round it twice. This means that the list describing a four-sided shape will have eight lists in it. The virtue of this is that when you are looking for the edge to start from, you will definitely find it in the first half of the description. Copying all but one edge of the figure, from that one on, will not result in you meeting the end of the list and having to jump back to the beginning. Expressing this in a symbolic form, imagine that you have two shapes each with four sides. Their list descriptions can be viewed as

[e1 e2 e3 e4 e1 e2 e3 e4]

and

[E1 E2 E3 E4 E1 E2 E3 E4]

where each element is actually a list, with two elements. If edge e3 of the first shape is to be joined to edge E2 of the second shape, and e3 and E2 have the same length, then the result will have edges

e1, e2(new angle), E3, E4, E1(new angle), e1

and the list description can be formed by joining the list with these elements to itself, using SENTENCE. The result is not so neat if the edges to be joined have different lengths. In such a case there will remnants of one or both of the two edges and these will need to be included in the description. You will also need to devise a suitable way of expressing exactly how the two edges are to be joined.

Your procedure for joining two shapes must also take into account two special cases. One is made obvious by the observation that joining two squares of equal size gives you a rectangle with four sides rather than a six sided shape. The other is when one or both shapes have concave bits. Joining along two of the concave edges may not be possible, but you should be able to convince yourself that if you try to do this, then the turning angle at one of the joining points will be greater than 360 degrees. This needs to be detected by the procedure, and treated as an error.

This project is one of the most elaborate in this chapter. It takes time to do well.

7.2 OPEN-ENDED PROJECTS

The projects outlined here can be take you in many different directions. They have no 'ultimate' goal.

7.2.1 **Mazes**

There are several types of mechanical turtle in the world, and some have touch sensors so that they can be programmed to avoid obstacles and explore their surroundings. This project aims to make similar things happen on the screen. In particular, the aim is to get the turtle to explore a maze drawn by the user.

The principal problem is that there is no way for the turtle to detect lines drawn on the screen. The solution proposed here is to have two representations of the maze, which agree but are independent. The maze will be made out of squares 10 units on a side, as shown in figure 7.8. There will also be a list showing where the walls of the maze are. The turtle will be able to tell if it has hit a wall on the screen by checking its co-ordinates to see which square it is in, and seeing if that square is in the list. An easy way to identify a square is by the co-ordinates of the bottom left corner, or rather by a relative displacement from the bottom left corner of the whole maze. An example will make this clearer: suppose that the bottom left corner of the maze is at

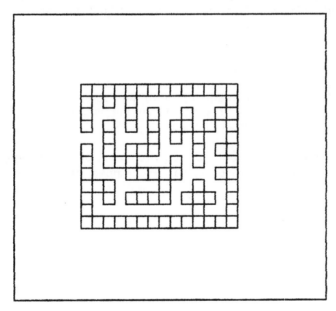

Figure 7.8

X=−80, Y=−60. If a square of the maze wall has its bottom left corner at X=−20, Y=30, then the X displacement is +60, the Y displacement is +90. The square can therefore be identified by the list [6 9], and the turtle can tell if it is in this square by seeing if the expression

```
LIST QUOTIENT (XCOR - (-80)) 10
     QUOTIENT (YCOR - (-60)) 10
```

is equal to [6 9]; this works because QUOTIENT outputs the integer part of the division, so the turtle's X co-ordinate can be anywhere between −20 and −10, its Y co-ordinate can be anywhere between 30 and 39 and the list output by the expression will be the same.

It seems at first sight as though it will be very tedious to set up the two representations. The task can be made very easy by defining a small 'maze editor' which allows the user to draw the maze and construct the list at the same time. In the following definitions, the variable WALL is where the list description is kept, and the editor is the procedure MAKEMAZE. It does some initial setting up and then invokes MAP to map out the maze according to keys pressed by the user:

```
key L    = move 1 square left
key R    = move 1 square right
key U    = move 1 square up the screen
key D    = move 1 square down the screen
key S    = include this square in the list, and draw it
key Q    = quit from the editor
```

Here are the procedures. The co-ordinates of the bottom left of the whole maze are recorded as the values of the variables MX and MY:

```
TO SQUARE
SETX XCOR + 10
SETY YCOR + 10
SETX XCOR - 10
SETY XCOR - 10
MAKE "WALL LPUT LIST QUOTIENT XCOR -
     :MX 10 QUOTIENT YCOR - :MY 10
     :WALL
END

TO MAP
MAKE "K READCHARACTER
IF :K = "L THEN PU SETX XCOR - 10
IF :K = "R THEN PU SETX XCOR + 10
IF :K = "U THEN PU SETY YCOR + 10
```

```
IF :K = "D THEN PU SETY YCOR - 10
IF :K = "S THEN PD SQUARE
IF :K = "Q THEN TOPLEVEL
MAP
END

TO MAKEMAZE
MAKE "MX ( - 80 )
MAKE "MY ( - 60 )
MAKE "WALL []
PU SETXY :MX :MY
SETH 45
MAP
END
```

The SETH 45 near the end of MAKEMAZE ensures that the turtle is pointing into the square whose bottom left corner it is standing on. This helps the user to know where the square will be drawn if he presses 'S' when using the editor. A useful addition might be a key to allow the user to delete a drawn square, and remove the details of it from the list.

The following procedure shows how the turtle can be made to grope around the maze at random. The turtle starts where it was left by the maze editor. It draws in pen colour 6, the inverting colour, so that it can wipe out its own tracks if it needs to retreat and so that it does not delete parts of the maze walls. To run it, give the command START:

```
TO START
PU
SETXY XCOR + 5 YCOR + 5
PD
PC 6
GROPE
END

TO GROPE
SETH 90 * RANDOM 4
FD 10
IF MEMBER? LIST QUOTIENT XCOR - :MX 10
     QUOTIENT YCOR - :MY 10 :WALL
     THEN BK 10
IF RC? THEN STOP ELSE GROPE
END
```

The SETXY in START puts the turtle in the middle of a square. In GROPE, the SETH gives the turtle a heading randomly chosen from 0, 90, 180, 270. The last line checks to see if the user has typed anything – typing any key stops the search.

Although it may seem as though almost all the work has been done for you, this is in fact just the beginning. The main work of the project is to get the turtle to explore the maze in a sensible way. One way to start is to get the turtle to record its path as it explores. This might be as a list of 'F's, 'L's and 'R's representing the FORWARDs, LEFTs and RIGHTs it has taken to get to its current position, or as a list representing the squares it has traversed. If you adopt the 'FLR' form, the thing to do is to update the path list first, then make the move, so that if the move turns out to land the turtle in the wall it has the information about how to get out.

The major hurdle is to cope with mazes that have 'islands', parts which are not connected to the outside walls of the maze. A dumb turtle could happily walk around the outside of an 'island' for ever, not realising the fact. To overcome this the turtle must have a means of knowing where it has been, so that it can tell whether it has visited the current square some time in the past.

An interesting experiment is to make the turtle explore in a limited way. It can follow alleys for a certain distance, and give up if it has not found turnings by then. If it fails to find the way out, it can then return to explore those alleys further. This is based on the assumption that many mazes have long blind alleys.

It is possible to speed up searching if you let the turtle 'teleport', using SETXY. This implies that the turtle must record suitable places to leap back to, as it explores. An advantage is that the turtle will not erase its tracks when it teleports, and so there will be a complete record on the screen of where it has searched.

7.2.2 Language Programs

There is a wide variety of possibilities for LOGO procedure sets which work with language. This section only hints at the possibilities, the idea being to give you enough to get yourself started.

The first idea is to try playing about with synonyms of words. It is entertaining, and can be instructive, to try recasting sentences using synonyms for various of the words in them and to see if the sense changes. The recasting of a sentence ought to be done under the user's control, by means of a simple sentence editor including commands such as 'replace the fifth word by a synonym if possible', 'replace all adjectives by synonyms' and so on. The LOGO procedure SPIN defined below is not so elaborate; all it does it to replace every word in a given sentence by a synonym if possible. For example,

```
PRINT SPIN [THE BIG BUT DUMB DOG
        WAS BITTEN BY THE SMALL BUT
        CLEVER CAT]
```

might print

```
THE LARGE BUT DOPEY CANINE WAS
BITTEN BY THE TINY BUT SMART CAT
```

The synonyms are provided as a list of lists:

```
MAKE "SYNL [[BIG LARGE HUGE GIANT VAST]
        [SMALL TINY WEE MINUTE] [INTELLIGENT
        CLEVER BRAINY SMART] [DUMB STUPID
        THICK DOPEY BRAINLESS] [FAT ADIPOSE
        PODGY HEFTY] [DOG CANINE POOCH]]
```

The definition of SPIN and its subprocedures are

```
TO SPIN :SENT
IF :SENT=[] THEN OUTPUT []
OUTPUT FPUT (SYN FIRST :SENT :SYNL )
        (SPIN BUTFIRST :SENT )
END

TO SYN :WORD :SLIST
IF :SLIST=[] THEN OUTPUT :WORD
IF MEMBER? :WORD FIRST :SLIST THEN
        OUTPUT RANDLIST FIRST :SLIST
OUTPUT SYN :WORD BUTFIRST :SLIST
END

TO RANDLIST :L
OUTPUT ITEM 1 + RANDOM COUNT :L :L
END
```

The job of RANDLIST is to output a random element of the list it receives as input. The procedure SYN takes a word and a list of synonym lists, and tries to find the word in one of those lists. If found, it outputs a random element of that list. If no list containing the word is found, it just outputs the word because it is then the only available synonym for itself.

Another useful procedure is INSERT, which inserts an element between two adjacent items in a list. It can be used as the basis of a simple sentence editor, allowing the user to do such things as insert extra adjectives and adverbs. Its counterpart, DELETE, can be defined in a similar way. INSERT expects three inputs: the item to insert, the list in which it is to be inserted, and the number of the element after which it is to be inserted. Items are numbered from 1, so INSERTing after item 0 is equivalent to putting the new item at the start.

```
TO INSERT :EL :L :NUM
IF :N=0 THEN OUTPUT FPUT :EL :L
OUTPUT FPUT FIRST :L INSERT :EL BF :L
     :NUM - 1
END
```

There are many word games which can be turned into LOGO procedures. The game 'Hangman' requires the the user to guess the letters which spell an unknown word, with only seven mistakes allowed. If a letter is guessed correctly, the player is told all the positions within the word where it appears. A game like 'Hangman' is hard to do well, because it depends on having a reasonably sized dictionary of words from which to choose the mystery word to spell. An arithmetic version is possible, in which the idea is to guess the numbers and operations which make up a specified equation, because it is possible to generate correct equations. An interesting variation is 'Textman', in which the idea is to guess the words which make up a mystery sentence. This depends on some of the grammatical ideas described below. Another entertaining game is 'Aunt Hettie Likes'. The idea is for the user to ask questions of the form

DOES SHE LIKE ‹something›

The reply depends on the application of a secret rule: the classic one is that Auntie Hettie likes anything that has a double letter in it. The aim is to guess the secret rule. Two players could take turns to devise a LOGO procedure, with a standard name such as RULE, that takes a word as input and outputs TRUE or FALSE appropriately. There are many variants of this idea, such as guessing the verb in a sentence, cracking a code, or predicting the next item in a linguistic or arithmetic sequence.

It is possible to write LOGO procedures to check whether a given sentence complies with a limited subset of English grammar. One way to specify the grammar is like this:

```
MAKE "SENTENCE.FORM
     [[NOUN.PHRASE VERB NOUN.PHRASE]
      [NOUN.PHRASE INTRANSITIVE.VERB]]

MAKE "NOUN.PHRASE.FORM
     [[DETERMINER NOUN]
      [DETERMINER ADJ NOUN]]

MAKE "DETERMINER.FORM [A THE]
MAKE "NOUN.FORM [DOG ELEPHANT BAKER
```

```
        SAUSAGE]
MAKE "VERB.FORM [ATE LIKED PAINTED]
MAKE "INTRANSITIVE.VERB.FORM [FAINTED]
MAKE "ADJ.FORM [GREEN BIG SWEATY]
```

The way to tell whether an item in a list, such as DOG, is meant to be an ordinary word or the name of a grammatical construction, is to check what

```
THING? WORD "DOG "'.FORM'
```

outputs. If it is TRUE then DOG is the name of a construction, if it is FALSE then it is just a word and nothing more. The task of checking whether the sentence

```
THE BIG SWEATY DOG ATE THE BAKER
```

fits the mini-grammar is almost identical in concept to the task of searching a maze.

7.2.3 A Database

This project involves some sophisticated points of list programming, and can be taken a very long way. It also introduces some rudimentary ideas of Artificial Intelligence. The aim is to create a database package. The basic definitions below provide four useful procedures:

SETUP This sets up the system.

FACT   This takes a list as input, recording that as a fact.

FACTS This takes no input, and prints the list of facts nicely.

QUERY This takes a list as input, and prints any known fact that matches it. The input can have elements that begin with a question mark, and these are taken to match anything at all.

The sample session using these procedures should give you the idea:

```
?FACT [FRED LIKES HAGGIS]
OK
?FACT [FRED HATES BEANS AND BEER]
OK
?FACT [HAGGIS IS CHEAP]
```

```
OK
?FACT [WALTER LIKES HAGGIS]
OK
?FACT [WALTER LIKES WHISKY]
OK
?FACT [WALTER LIKES WALTER]
OK
?FACTS
--- FRED LIKES HAGGIS
--- FRED HATES BEANS AND BEER
--- HAGGIS IS CHEAP
--- WALTER LIKES HAGGIS
--- WALTER LIKES WHISKY
--- WALTER LIKES WALTER
?QUERY [FRED LIKES ?X]
FRED LIKES HAGGIS
?QUERY [?X LIKES HAGGIS]
FRED LIKES HAGGIS
WALTER LIKES HAGGIS
?QUERY [?THIS LIKES ?THAT]
FRED LIKES HAGGIS
WALTER LIKES HAGGIS
WALTER LIKES WHISKY
WALTER LIKES WALTER
?QUERY [FRED HATES ?X]
... NO MATCH
?QUERY [FRED HATES ?A AND ?B]
FRED HATES BEANS AND BEER
?QUERY [?A LIKES ?A]
WALTER LIKES WALTER
```

In each case, all the facts that precisely match the query are printed. Note the last case, in which the goal is to find something that likes itself; the 'database variable' ?A turns up twice in the query.

The facts are held as a list of lists, the value of a variable called FACTS. LOGO does not object that this is also the name of a procedure. The definitions of SETUP, FACT and FACTS are very simple:

```
TO SETUP
MAKE "FACTS []
END

TO FACT :L
MAKE "FACTS LPUT :L :FACTS
END

TO FACTS
IF :FACTS=[] THEN PRINT [... NO FACTS]
     ELSE PRINTFACTS :FACTS
```

```
END

TO PRINTFACTS :L
IF :L=[] THEN STOP
PRINT1 "'--- '"
PRINT FIRST :L
PRINTFACTS BUTFIRST :L
END
```

The definition of QUERY is fairly short but much more sophisticated. QUERY invokes a procedure called SCAN to look for matches in the list of facts. SCAN works through the list of facts, applying MATCH? to see if the query matches each fact in turn. The procedure MATCH? takes two inputs – the first is the query, the second is one fact from the list of them. It works recursively.

```
TO QUERY :Q
MAKE "NOMATCH "TRUE
SCAN :Q :FACTS
IF :NOMATCH THEN PRINT [... NO MATCH]
END

TO SCAN :QUERY :FACTS
IF :FACTS=[] THEN STOP
IF MATCH? :QUERY (FIRST :FACTS ) THEN
      PRINT FIRST :FACTS
SCAN :QUERY (BUTFIRST :FACTS )
END

TO MATCH? :Q :FACT
IF ALLOF (:Q=[] ) (:FACT=[] ) THEN
      MAKE "NOMATCH "FALSE OUTPUT "TRUE
IF FIRST FIRST :Q = "? THEN MAKE "Q
      REPLACE FIRST :Q FIRST :FACT :Q
IF NOT (FIRST :Q ) = (FIRST :FACT )
      THEN OUTPUT "FALSE
OUTPUT MATCH? BUTFIRST :Q BUTFIRST :FACT
END
```

The REPLACE procedure used in MATCH? is the one defined in section 4.5.4. The inputs are, in order, the element to be replaced throughout the list, the element to replace it by, and the list itself. If MATCH? finds an element of the query which begins with a question mark, it replaces all occurrences of that element in the rest of the query by the corresponding element from the fact being examined, before proceeding to check the match. If this is confusing, work through some of the examples from the sample session above, on paper.

There are many ways this embryo package can be extended. One possibility is to alter FACT to allow 'input inferences'. The idea is to define a new procedure, say INFER, that will allow the user to command the package to make certain inferences when FACT is used in future. For example, the command

INFER [?X LIKES HAGGIS] [?X IS SCOTTISH]

should be taken to mean that, if a fact 'someone likes haggis' is entered, then the fact 'the person is Scottish' should be entered automatically. INFER need only update a list of lists, each of which consists of the two inputs from an INFER command. This list can then be used by FACT, which should check whether the fact matches the first input to any previous INFER. If it does, the corresponding second input should be treated as the input to a new use of FACT, so that after these commands

INFER [?X EATS HAGGIS] [?X IS SCOTTISH]
INFER [?A IS SCOTTISH] [?A HAS A KILT]
FACT [DONALD EATS HAGGIS]

the facts [DONALD EATS HAGGIS], [DONALD IS SCOTTISH] and [DONALD HAS A KILT] are all included in the FACTS list.

A severe test of your programming skill is to amend QUERY to allow conjunctions of queries, for example

QUERY [[?Z LIKES ?Y] [?Y IS CHEAP]]

should print (assuming the facts in the sample session)

FRED LIKES HAGGIS
HAGGIS IS CHEAP
WALTER LIKES HAGGIS
HAGGIS IS CHEAP

and nothing else. The hurdle is producing a new version of MATCH?. It must know the entire query, not just one component of it. To illustrate the problem: suppose the new MATCH? has been trying to match [?Z LIKES ?Y] with [FRED LIKES WHISKY], and has reached the stage of matching [?Y] with [WHISKY] in its recursing. Then it must go on to examine whether there is any match for the fact [WHISKY IS CHEAP], and return to examining the previous part of the query when it finds none. Of course, it should be equally possible to conjoin three or more parts for a single query.

A further refinement is to attach probability values to facts, and have QUERY print a probability value for each answer to a conjunction.

7.2.4 Simple Pattern Recognition

Many so-called 'intelligence tests' in books and newspapers ask for the answers to questions such as this:

Give the next term in the sequence –

A B A B D D C F G ...

The first step is to recognise that the letters are grouped in threes. To generate the next three, the rule is to update the first of the three by one letter, the second by two and the third by three. If the question were to find the next term in the sequence

1 2 1 2 4 4 3 6 7 ...

it would be much easier to recognise the arithmetic progression 121, 244, 367 .. in disguise. You can write LOGO procedures to analyse such questions to determine the pattern. The approach is to try values from 1 upward for the length of the group, and see whether there is some arithmetic progression visible. With a letter sequence, the letters can be turned into numbers by using the procedure ASCII: the letter sequence given above would be

65 66 65 66 68 68 67 70 71 ...

Split into lists of length three, this gives three lists representing numbers in base 1000 (say), and the procedures you produced for the project in section 5.3.6 can be used to check whether this forms an arithmetic progression. Since at least three terms are needed to confirm that the pattern is an arithmetic progression, the LOGO procedure can safely give up if the length of the group reaches one third of the length of the given sequence without finding a progression.

Sometimes letter sequences assume that the alphabet wraps round from Z back to A. In this case you need to be looking for an arithmetic progression using arithmetic modulo 26.

7.2.5 Games

There are vasts number of games. They fall into three groups:

(a)   those in which you play the machine

(b)   those in which you play someone else, and the machine
        referees

(c)   those in which the machine acts as board or dice or
        rulebook.

Those in category (a) tend to be simple. There are many variants
of games such as tic-tac-toe, fox-and-geese and other easy
board games for which you can write LOGO procedures to play
you. They nearly all suffer from the same fault, which is that you
know how the machine plays. Games with an element of chance
are more fun to play – consult a book of games for ideas. The
simplest are games such as 'Shoot' where the turtle lies near one
corner of the screen, a slowly animated target moves near the
other corner and you have to guess a range and heading to get
the turtle to hit the target. Variants such as 'turtle golf', with
many targets to be hit in sequence, naturally follow from this.

Category (b) offers a very wide scope. Competitive versions
of one-person games like 'Shoot' are usually possible. At the
other end of the scale of difficulty, there are very elaborate
games such as 'Kriegspiel'. This is chess, but neither player can
see his opponent's pieces, and has to try moves in the dark.
Normally there is a referee, who announces check when it happens, and removes pieces (without naming them to the capturer)
as appropriate, and checks on the legality of moves. You may find
it possible (but difficult) to write LOGO procedures to act as
referee, showing each player his own pieces when it is his turn
and erasing them when it is not.

Category (c) is dull. There are few games in which the
record-keeping powers of a computer really make a difference. Do
not let that stop you trying to invent ones, though.

7.3 BEYOND LOGO

Now you know LOGO. Nobody can claim to know all there is to
know about it, because it is constantly developing as a language.
The last project in this book is to attempt to invent further
features, or even redesign LOGO. The criteria to use in judging
changes are their usefulness and comprehensibility.

To get you started, the FOR command is defined below. It is
used in the following way. The command

    FOR "Z IN [10 25 100] [BOX :Z RT 10]

is equivalent to

```
BOX  10  RT  10
BOX  25  RT  10
BOX  100  RT  10
```

The definition is

```
TO  FOR  :QXRY  :IN.VALUE  :L  :COMM
IF  :L=[]  THEN  STOP
IF  NOT  :IN.VALUE  =  "OUTPUT.BY.IN  THEN
        ERROR  [MISSING  KEYWORD:  IN]
MAKE  :QXRY  FIRST  :L
REPEAT  1  :COMM
FOR  :QXRY  :IN.VALUE  BF  :L  :COMM
END

TO  IN
OUTPUT  "OUTPUT.BY.IN
END
```

The procedure IN is included purely to make the FOR command easier to read when used in procedures. FOR can be improved in many ways. For example, as it stands, the command

```
FOR  "X  IN  [PRINT  FORWARD]  [:X  100]
```

will not work. This is because

```
REPEAT  1  [:X  100]
```

will not work, as the elements inside the list are not a legal command. A solution is to use the REPLACE procedure defined in section 4.5.4, to replace all occurrences of a colon followed by the word given as first input to FOR by the value of the variable named by that word.

Many people also want a means of adding comments in a procedure. The cheap answer is

```
TO  COMMENT  :L
END
```

so that comments in procedures will look like this:

```
    ...
FD  100
COMMENT  [SENDS  THE  TURTLE  FORWARD]
    ...
```

As well as annotating your procedures in this way, you should also cultivate the habit of writing down your procedures and keeping them with your other LOGO notes – in a loose leaf binder, say. That way you can also note down such points as why you did something in a particular way, and what the problems and potential improvements are.

7.4 IN CONCLUSION

Computing can be a social activity. The best way to find new ideas and new projects is to discuss them with other people, in competition or in co-operation. Try brainstorming sessions, to explore a project or devise a method of representation. Form groups and get them into friendly competition. Don't restrict yourself to LOGO; look at other people's programs in other languages for their ideas, and give them some of your own. If you create something you're really proud of, then tell others about it or send it to one of the many magazines.

Enjoy it!

Appendix A
Terrapin LOGO

A.1 Terrapin LOGO

This appendix describes the Terrapin LOGO language used in the main body of this book and which runs on the Apple II. Terrapin LOGO is sold by

> Terrapin Inc.,
> 380 Green Street,
> Cambridge,
> Massachusetts 02139, USA.

A.2 Conventions

Conventions description uses the following sort of notation:

FORWARD (FD)	n
BUTFIRST (BF)	nwl => nwl
PRINT	nwl...
LIST	nwl nwl... => l

meaning

(a)   FORWARD can be abbreviated to FD, and it expects a number as input

(b)   BUTFIRST can be abbreviated to BF, it expects a number, word or list as input and it outputs a number, word or list.

(c)   PRINT expects a number, word or list as input, and it can be greedy

(d)   LIST normally expects two inputs, each a number, word or list, and outputs a list, but it can be greedy.

The abbreviations used are

n   number
w   word
l   list
t   truth value, the word TRUE or the word FALSE

A.3 Turtle Graphics

The screen is 280 turtle units wide and 240 turtle units high. The origin of co-ordinates is at the middle of the screen. When the turtle has a heading of 0 degrees it is pointing straight up the screen. The heading increases as the turtle turns clockwise.

FORWARD (FD)   n

BACK (BK)   n

LEFT (LT)   n
            In degrees.

RIGHT (RT)   n
            In degrees

HOME

CLEARSCREEN (CS)

DRAW
            Initialises the drawing.

NODRAW
            Destroys any drawing and reverts to using the screen only for text.

WRAP
            After this command, if the turtle leaves one edge of the screen it reappears at the other.

NOWRAP
            After this command, the turtle is not allowed to cross the edges of the screen.

SETX   n

SETY   n

SETHEADING (SETH)   n
          Sets the heading to be in the range 0-360 degrees.

SETXY   n n
          All these draw a line if the pen is down.

PENDOWN (PD)

PENUP (PU)

PENCOLOR (PC)   n
          The input must be an integer in the range 0-6.

BACKGROUND (BG)   n
          Like PENCOLOR, but sets the background color.

SHOWTURTLE (ST)

HIDETURTLE (HT)

FULLSCREEN

SPLITSCREEN

XCOR   => n

YCOR   => n

HEADING   => n

TOWARDS   n n => n
          The inputs are the x and y of a point on the screen.
          The output is a heading towards that point, in
          degrees.

TURTLESTATE   => l
          The output list has four elements: the first is TRUE
          or FALSE depending on whether the pen is down, the
          second is TRUE or FALSE depending on whether the
          turtle is shown or hidden, the third is the pen color
          and the last is the background color.

A.4 Arithmetic

Numbers can be given in various forms:

    35
    3.6
    3.7E2   meaning 370
    3.8N2   meaning 0.038

There can be a minus sign at the front; there should be no

space between the minus and the first digit. LOGO can work with integers in the range −2147483648 to 2147483647, with complete accuracy. Otherwise LOGO only works to around seven significant figures, although it can cope with numbers having up to 38 digits on either side of the decimal point, with some loss of accuracy.

+, −, *, /	n n => n

These four are used in a conventional way: 3 + 4, not + 3 4. Use parentheses to avoid ambiguity.

SIN	n => n

COS	n => n

ATAN	n n => n

Outputs the angle, in degrees between 0 and 360, whose arctangent is the first input divided by the second.

SQRT	n => n

INTEGER	n => n

Removes any fractional part.

ROUND	n => n

Rounds the input to the nearest integer.

QUOTIENT	n n => n

Rounds its inputs, outputs the integer quotient of them.

REMAINDER	n n => n

Rounds its inputs, outputs the remainder on dividing first input by second.

RANDOM	n => n

Rounds its input, then outputs a random integer in the range 0 to one less than the input.

RANDOMIZE

Makes the sequence of numbers generated by repeated use of RANDOM unpredictable. Without RANDOMIZE, the sequence would be the same each time the computer is turned on.

A.5 Procedures

TO	w

Input is NOT quoted.

EDIT	w

Input is NOT quoted

DEFINE   w l

The first input is a name (it IS quoted), the second
is a list of lists defining a procedure to be known by
that name.

TEXT   w => l

Input is a name (it IS quoted). Output is a list of
lists, giving the definition of the procedure named.

ERASE (ER)   w

The input is NOT quoted. Makes LOGO forget about
the named procedure. Can also use the qualifiers
PROCEDURES, NAMES (for all variable names) or ALL
(both NAMES and PROCEDURES).

A.6 Words and Lists

FIRST   nwl => nwl

LAST   nwl => nwl

BUTFIRST (BF)   nwl => nwl

BUTLAST (BL)   nwl => nwl

LIST   nwl nwl... => l

SENTENCE (SE)   nwl nwl... => l

Like LIST, but input lists get broken into the collection of separate elements first.

FPUT   nwl l => l

Puts the first input onto the front of the list.

LPUT   nwl l => l

Puts the first input onto the end of the list.

WORD   nw nw... => nw

Concatenates its inputs.

A.7 Condition Procedures

IF t THEN ...

IF t THEN ... ELSE ...

TEST t

IFTRUE ... (IFT)

IFFALSE ... (IFF)

>, <	n n => t

Used in the customary way: 2 > 1, not > 2 1.

=	nwl nwl => t

Used in the customary way: 2 = 2, not = 2 2.

LIST?	nwl => t
WORD?	nwl => t
NUMBER?	nwl => t
THING?	nwl => t

Outputs TRUE if the input is the name of an existing variable.

ALLOF	t t... => t
ANYOF	t t... => t
NOT	t => t

A.8 Control

STOP

TOPLEVEL

OUTPUT (OP)	nwl
REPEAT	n l
RUN	l

Like REPEAT 1 ...

GO	w

Transfers control to the line labelled with the given word. To label a line, start it with the word, followed immediately (no space) by a colon.

A.9 Screen Input/Output

PRINT (PR)	nwl...
PRINT1	nwl...

Like PRINT, but does not move on to a new line after printing.

REQUEST (RQ)	=> l

READCHARACTER (RC) => w

Outputs a single-character word consisting of the least recent character typed but not yet read.

RC?   => t

Outputs TRUE if there are characters that have been typed but not read.

CLEARINPUT

Causes any characters typed but not so far read to be thrown away.

CLEARTEXT

Erases any text on the screen.

CURSOR   n n

Positions the cursor at the given column (0-39) and row (0-23). Top left is 0,0.

ASCII   nw => n

The input must be one character (perhaps a single-digit number). Outputs the ASCII code of that character.

CHAR   n => nw

The reverse of ASCII.

PADDLE   n => n

The input must be one of 0, 1, 2 or 3, specifying a paddle. The output is in the range 0-255, depending on that paddle setting.

PADDLEBUTTON   n => t

The input must be one of 0, 1, or 2, specifying a paddle. The output is TRUE if the button on that paddle is being pressed.

OUTDEV   n

The input is an integer. If it is in the range 1-8, it is taken to specify a slot to which output should be sent, rather than the screen. If it is larger than 8, it is taken as the entry address of an assembly language routine that will handle all output. The key CTRL-SHIFT-M restores the method of outputting to the default arrangement.

A.10 **Variables**

MAKE   w nwl"

THING (:)   w => nwl

The colon is not a true abbreviation – see the comments in chapter 2.

ERNAME   w

Makes LOGO forget about the named variable.

A.11 Information

CATALOG

PRINTOUT (PO)   w

Can also take the qualifiers ALL, NAMES, TITLES or PROCEDURES. POTS is short for PO TITLES.

A.12 Files

SAVE   w

Saves everything but the drawing in the named file.

READ   w

Reads in the contents of the named file.

ERASEFILE   w

SAVEPICT   w

Saves the drawing in the named file.

READPICT   w

Reads in the drawing in the named file.

ERASEPICT   w

A.13 Tracing

TRACE

The key CTRL-Z causes a pause.

NOTRACE

PAUSE

Causes a pause, during which any commands can be given.

CONTINUE (CO)

Resumes activity, ends a pause.

A.14 Editing Keys

Any normal text you type is inserted, without overwriting any existing text. The following keys are used for editing. Most can be used outside the editor too.

ESC   Rubs out the character to the left of the cursor.

CTRL-D Rubs out the character on which the cursor is standing.

← → Moves the cursor left or right.

CTRL-A Moves the cursor to the start of the current line of LOGO (maybe not the current screen line).

CTRL-E Moves the cursor to the end of the current line of LOGO (maybe not the current screen line).

CTRL-K Deletes all characters to the right of the cursor on the current line of LOGO.

CTRL-N (Editor only) Moves the cursor down to the next line of LOGO.

CTRL-P (Editor) Moves the cursor up to the previous line of LOGO. (Normal) Retypes the previous line, unless it included a REPEAT or RUN.

CTRL-O (Editor only) Splices in a blank line after the current line of LOGO.

CTRL-B (Editor) Moves the cursor back through the definition by about a screenful.

CTRL-F (Editor) Moves the cursor on through the definition by about a screenful. (Normal) Full graphics screen, no text displayed.

CTRL-L (Editor only) Moves the definition so that the current line is near the middle of the screen.

CTRL-C (Editor only) Completes the editing.

CTRL-G (Editor) Aborts the editing. (Normal) Aborts the command.

A.15 **Other Special Keys**

SHIFT-N Left square bracket ('[').

SHIFT-M Right square bracket (']').

CTRL-SHIFT-P Underscore ('_').

CTRL-G Aborts the command.

CTRL-Z Causes a pause.

CTRL-W Suspends LOGO command and output. Typing anything causes the command and outputting to resume.

CTRL-F Full graphics screen, no text displayed.

CTRL-S Mixed text and graphics. Four lines of text displayed.

CTRL-T No graphics displayed. Twenty four lines of text displayed.

A.16 Special Commands

.ASPECT   n

The input is a number representing the ratio of the size of a unit vertical step to the size of a unit horizontal step. Normally it is 0.8, but you may need to change it if circles look elliptical on your screen. Changing it changes the permissible range of y coordinate values.

.BPT

Jumps into the Apple monitor. You can get back to LOGO by typing G or CTRL-Y.

.CALL   n

The input should be an integer. Calls the assembly language subroutine at that address.

.DEPOSIT   n n

The first input is an address in memory, the second is a value. Like BASIC's POKE.

.EXAMINE   n => n

Outputs the value at the given memory address. Like BASIC's PEEK.

DOS   l

Passes the command to the Apple DOS monitor.

Appendix B
Apple LOGO

B.1 Apple LOGO

This appendix describes the Apple LOGO language, as sold by

Apple Computer Inc.,
10260 Bandley Drive,
Cupertino,
California 95014, USA.

Apple LOGO is very like Terrapin LOGO in many ways, but there are some traps for the careless. These are pointed out in the notes that follow.

B.2 Conventions

The description uses the notation described in section A.1. One further abbreviation is used; it is

    P   word naming a package (see notes below).

B.3 Turtle Graphics

The screen is 280 turtle units wide and 240 turtle units high. The origin of co-ordinates is at the middle of the screen. When the turtle has a heading of 0 degrees it is pointing straight up the screen. The heading increases as the turtle turns clockwise.

FORWARD (FD)   n

BACK (BK)   n

LEFT (LT)   n
        In degrees.

RIGHT (RT)   n
        In degrees

HOME

CLEAN

        Terrapin LOGO CLEARSCREEN. Clears the drawing, does not affect the turtle.

CLEARSCREEN (CS)
        Different from Terrapin LOGO; equivalent to DRAW.

WRAP

        After this command, if the turtle leaves one edge of the screen it reappears at the other.

FENCE

        Terrapin LOGO NOWRAP. After this command, the turtle is not allowed to cross the edges of the screen.

WINDOW

        No Terrapin LOGO equivalent. Makes the display behave like a window onto the centre of a huge drawing area. No wrapping.

SETX   n

SETY   n

SETHEADING (SETH)   n
        Sets the heading to be in the range 0–360 degrees.

SETPOS   l
        Takes a list of two numbers, an x and a y. Similar to Terrapin LOGO SETXY.

PENDOWN (PD)

PENUP (PU)

SETPC   n
        Terrapin LOGO PENCOLOR. Sets the pen color (0–5). To get the reversing color use PENREVERSE.

PENCOLOR (PC)   => n
        Different from Terrapin LOGO. Outputs the pen color.

PENREVERSE
        Sets the pen to the reversing color.

PENERASE
        Sets the pen to the background color.

SETBG   n
                          Terrapin LOGO BACKGROUND. Sets the background
                          color (0-5 only).

BACKGROUND (BG)   => n
                          Different from Terrapin LOGO. Outputs the background
                          color.

SHOWTURTLE (ST)

HIDETURTLE (HT)

FULLSCREEN

SPLITSCREEN

TEXTSCREEN
                          Terrapin LOGO NODRAW.

XCOR   => n

YCOR   => n

HEADING   => n

TOWARDS   n n => n
                          The inputs are the x and y of a point on the screen.
                          The output is a heading towards that point, in
                          degrees.

PEN   => l
                          No Terrapin LOGO equivalent. Outputs a list of two
                          elements, the first being one of PENDOWN, PENUP,
                          PENERASE or PENREVERSE, and the second being
                          the pen color (an integer).

SETPEN   l
                          Sets the pen state - see PEN.

SHOWNP   => t
                          Outputs TRUE if the turtle is being shown, FALSE if
                          hidden.

B.4 Arithmetic

Numbers can be given in various forms:

    35
    3.6
    3.7E2   meaning 370
    3.8N2   meaning 0.038

The rules are exactly as for Terrapin LOGO (described in section

A.4).

+, −, *, /	n n => n

These four are used in a conventional way: 3 + 4, not + 3 4. Use parentheses to avoid ambiguity.

SIN	n => n

COS	n => n

ARCTAN	n n => n

Terrapin LOGO ATAN. Outputs the angle, in degrees between 0 and 360, whose arctangent is the first input divided by the second.

SQRT	n => n

INT	n => n

Terrapin LOGO INTEGER. Removes any fractional part.

ROUND	n => n

Rounds the input to the nearest integer.

QUOTIENT	n n => n

Rounds its inputs, outputs the integer quotient of them.

PRODUCT	n n... => n

SUM	n n... => n

REMAINDER	n n => n

Rounds its inputs, outputs the remainder on dividing first input by second.

RANDOM	n => n

Rounds its input, then outputs a random integer in the range 0 to one less than the input.

RERANDOM

Terrapin LOGO RANDOMIZE.

B.5 Procedures

In Apple LOGO, the input to TO, EDIT etc. is quoted.

TO	w

Input IS quoted.

EDIT	w

input IS quoted

DEFINE   w l

The first input is a name (it IS quoted), the second is a list of lists defining a procedure to be known by that name.

TEXT   w => l

Input is a name (it IS quoted). Output is a list of lists, giving the definition of the procedure named.

ERASE (ER)   wl

The input IS quoted. Makes LOGO forget about the named procedure(s).

ERPS

Erases all procedures not buried (see section B.10 on packages). Can also take a package name or a list of them as input, in which case the effect is confined to those packages.

B.6 Words and Lists

FIRST   nwl => nwl

LAST   nwl => nwl

BUTFIRST (BF)   nwl => nwl

BUTLAST (BL)   nwl => nwl

LIST   nwl nwl... => l

SENTENCE (SE)   nwl nwl... => l

Like LIST, but input lists get broken into the collection of separate elements first.

FPUT   nwl l => l

Puts the first input onto the front of the list.

LPUT   nwl l => l

Puts the first input onto the end of the list.

WORD   nw nw... => nw

Concatenates its inputs.

COUNT   l => n

Outputs the number of elements of the list. Does not accept a word as input.

ITEM   n l => nwl

Outputs the chosen element from the list.

B.7 Condition Procedures

The syntax of the IF command is a major difference between Apple LOGO and Terrapin LOGO. Apple LOGO also uses a final 'P' rather than a final '?' in naming the various condition testing procedures.

IF t l

IF t l l

> Apple LOGO's IF has a similarity to REPEAT. The one or two lists contain commands. If the condition is TRUE, the first is obeyed. The second list is only obeyed if the condition is FALSE.

TEST t

IFTRUE ... (IFT)

IFFALSE ... (IFF)

>, <   n n => t
> Used in the customary way: 2 > 1, not > 2 1.

=   nwl nwl => t
> Used in the customary way: 2 = 2, not = 2 2.

LISTP   nwl => t

WORDP   nwl => t

NUMBERP   nwl => t

EQUALP   nwl nwl => t

EMPTYP   wl => t
> Outputs TRUE if the input is the empty word or list.

MEMBERP   nwl l => t
> Outputs TRUE if the first input is a member of the list.

THINGP   nwl => t
> Outputs TRUE if the input is the name of an existing variable.

DEFINEDP   w => t
> Outputs TRUE if the input is the name of an existing procedure.

PRIMITIVEP   w => t
> Outouts TRUE if the input is the name of a built-in procedure.

AND   t t...   => t
                  Terrapin LOGO ALLOF.

OR   t t...   => t
                  Terrapin LOGO ANYOF.

NOT   t   => t

B.8 Control

In Apple LOGO the command THROW "TOPLEVEL is used instead of TOPLEVEL. There are two procedures, CATCH and THROW, for transferring control. Take an example:

    CATCH "FRED [PROC1 PROC2 PROC3]

causes the commands in the list to be obeyed. However, if in the course of obeying them LOGO meets the command

    THROW "FRED

then the CATCH command ends immediately. The LOGO system itself is repeatedly obeying the command

    CATCH "TOPLEVEL [your typed-in commands]

Another special case is that any error results in an implied

    THROW "ERROR

which you can CATCH if you want to provide your own error routines (see ERROR below).

STOP

OUTPUT (OP)   nwl

REPEAT   n l

RUN   l
                  Like REPEAT 1 ...

GO   w
                  Transfers control to the matching LABEL in the same procedure.

LABEL   w

CATCH   w l

THROW   w

ERROR

    Outputs information about the most recent error – see the technical manual for details.

B.9 Screen Input/Output

PRINT (PR)   nwl...

TYPE   nwl...

    Terrapin LOGO PRINT1. Like PRINT, but does not move on to a new line after printing.

SHOW   nwl

    Like PRINT, but also prints the outermost brackets of lists.

READLIST (RL)   => l

    Terrapin LOGO REQUEST.

READCHAR (RC)   => w

    Terrapin LOGO READCHARACTER. Outputs a single-character word consisting of the least recent character typed but not yet read.

KEYP   => t

    Terrapin LOGO RC?. Outputs TRUE if there are characters that have been typed but not read.

CLEARTEXT

    Erases any text on the screen.

SETCURSOR   l

    Similar to Terrapin LOGO CURSOR. The input is a list of two numbers. Positions the cursor at the given column (0–39) and row (0–23). Top left is 0,0.

CURSOR   => l

    Outputs a two element list giving the column and row of the cursor.

ASCII   nw => n

    The input must be one character (perhaps a single-digit number). Outputs the ASCII code of that character.

CHAR   n => nw

    The reverse of ASCII.

PADDLE   n => n

    The input must be one of 0, 1, 2 or 3, specifying a paddle. The output is in the range 0–255, depending on that paddle setting.

BUTTONP   n   =>   t

Terrapin LOGO PADDLEBUTTON. The input must be one of 0, 1, or 2, specifying a paddle. The output is TRUE if the button on that paddle is being pressed.

.PRINTER   n

Like Terrapin LOGO OUTDEV. The input is an integer. If it is in the range 1-8, it is taken to specify a slot to which output should be sent, rather than the screen. If it is in the range 9-15, output goes both to the screen and to slot (input - 8).

B.10 Packages

In Apple LOGO variables and procedures can be put into 'packages', and specified packages can be saved on disk or erased from memory.

PACKAGE   P   wl

The first input is the name of a package (if it is unknown this will make it known). The second input is a word, or a list of words, naming variables and procedures to be included in the package.

PKGALL   P

Packages everything not yet packaged.

BURY   P

Marks the contents of the package, so that they cannot be affected by POALL, ERALL, ERNS, ERPS, PONS, POPS, POTS or SAVE.

UNBURY   P

Undoes the effect of BURY.

B.11 Packages

MAKE   w   nwl

THING (:)   w   =>   nwl

The colon is not a true abbreviation - see the comments in chapter 2.

LOCAL   w

Creates a variable having the given name, which temporarily supercedes any other of the same name.

The variable ceases to exist when the procedure in which it was created by LOCAL comes to an end.

ERN   wl

Makes LOGO forget about the named variable(s).

ERNS

Erases all (unburied) variables. Can also take a package name, or a list of them, when it confines the effect to those packages.

B.12 Information

CATALOG

PO   wl

Prints out definitions of the named procedure(s).

PONS

Prints out the values of all (unburied) variables. Can take a package name as input, to confine printing to that package.

POPS

Prints out all (unburied) procedure definitions. Can take a package name as input, to confine printing to that package.

POALL

Combines PONS and POPS.

POTS

Prints out the titles of all (unburied) procedures. Can take a package name as input, to confine printing to that package.

B.13 Files

SAVE   w

Saves everything (unburied) except the drawing in the named file. Can take a second input – a package name or a list of them – to confine saving to those packages.

LOAD   w

Like Terrapin LOGO READ. Reads in the contents of the named file. Can also take a package name as a second input, and the file contents will then be loaded into that package.

ERASEFILE   w

B.14 Tracing

PAUSE

>Causes a pause, during which any commands can be given.

CO

>Terrapin LOGO CONTINUE. Resumes activity, ends a pause.

B.15 Editing Keys

Any normal text you type is inserted, without overwriting any existing text. The following keys are used for editing. Most can be used outside the editor too.

CTRL-D Rubs out the character on which the cursor is standing.

←   Rubs out the character to the left of the cursor.

→   Moves the cursor right.

CTRL-B Moves the cursor left.

CTRL-A Moves the cursor to the start of the current line of LOGO (maybe not the current screen line).

CTRL-E Moves the cursor to the end of the current line of LOGO (maybe not the current screen line).

CTRL-K Deletes all characters to the right of the cursor on the current line of LOGO.

CTRL-Y Inserts what was last deleted by CTRL-K.

CTRL-N (Editor only) Moves the cursor down to the next line of LOGO.

CTRL-P (Editor) Moves the cursor up to the previous line of LOGO. (Normal) Retypes the previous line, unless it included a REPEAT or RUN.

CTRL-O (Editor only) Splices in a blank line after the current line of LOGO.

ESC V (Editor) Moves the cursor back through the definition by about a screenful.

CTRL-V (Editor) Moves the cursor on through the definition by about a screenful.

CTRL-L (Editor only) Moves the definition so that the current line is near the middle of the screen. (Normal) Full graphics screen, no text.

CTRL-C (Editor only) Completes the editing.

CTRL-G (Editor) Aborts the editing. (Normal) Aborts the command.

ESC ‹ (Editor only) Moves the cursor to the start of all the text.

ESC › (Editor only) Moves the cursor to the end of all the text.

B.16 Other Special Keys

SHIFT-N Left square bracket ('[').

SHIFT-M Right square bracket (']').

CTRL-G Aborts the command.

CTRL-Z Causes a pause.

CTRL-W Suspends LOGO command and output. Typing anything causes the command and outputting to resume.

CTRL-L Full graphics screen, no text displayed.

CTRL-S Mixed text and graphics. Four lines of text displayed.

CTRL-T No graphics displayed. Twenty four lines of text displayed.

CTRL-Q Allows you to remove any special significance, as far as LOGO is concerned, from the next character typed in. The

CTRL-Q appears as a backslash.

B.17 Properties

In Apple LOGO, names (for instance, variable names or procedure names) can have properties associated with them. A property has a name and a value. You could construct such a feature for yourself using lists, but Apple LOGO provides various procedures for the sake of efficiency.

PPROP   w wl nwl

     The first input is a name, the second is a property name for that name, the third is the value of the named property.

GPROP   w wl => nwl

     The first input is a name, the second a property name. Outputs the value of the property.

PLIST   w => l

     Takes a name as input. Outputs a list of property names and values.

REMPROP   w wl

     Takes a name and a property name, and erases that property of the name.

PPS

     With no input, prints the properties of everything. Can take a package name or a list of packages, then confines its effect to those packages.

B.18 Special Commands

SETSCRUNCH   n

     Terrapin LOGO .ASPECT. The input is a number representing the ratio of the size of a unit vertical step to the size of a unit horizontal step. Normally it is 0.8, but you may need to change it if circles look elliptical on your screen. Changing it changes the permissible range of y co-ordinate values.

SCRUNCH   => n

     Outputs the current screen scaling.

.BPT

     Jumps into the Apple monitor. You can get back to LOGO by typing G or CTRL-Y.

.DEPOSIT   n n
The first input is an address in memory, the second is a value. Like BASIC's POKE.

.EXAMINE   n => n
Outputs the value at the given memory address. Like BASIC's PEEK.

SETDISK   inputs
Takes one to three inputs, to select a disk to use. The first input is the drive number, the (optional) second is the slot number and the (optional) third is the disk volume number.

DISK   => l
Outputs a list of three numbers – see SETDISK.

COPYDEF   w w
Causes the first input to name whatever the second input names.

Appendix C
TI LOGO

C.1 TI LOGO FOR THE TI-99/4a

This appendix describes the TI LOGO language for the TI-99/4a computer. The version for the TI-99/4 is almost identical. The difference between the two concerns the keyboard – the 99/4a has a FCTN key, used in a similar way to the SHIFT and CTRL keys. Various operations available on the 99/4a as FCTN-key combinations were provided as SHIFT-key combinations on the 99/4. TI LOGO is available from suppliers of Texas Instruments Inc. computer products.

TI LOGO differs from Terrapin LOGO and Apple LOGO in several important ways. While TI LOGO has generally similar turtle graphics, the list handling facilities are not quite as broad. The main difference is that TI LOGO has 'sprites' and 'tiles' as well as the turtle. Both are graphic objects. The sprites are used for animation; the turtle is normally controlled by commands affecting its heading and location, but sprites are normally controlled by commands affecting their heading, speed and visible shape. The 'tiles' are just the visible forms of the characters you normally see on the screen, such as the letters of the alphabet.

There are 32 sprites, numbered 0 to 31. Commands can be directed at one, several or all at once. There are 26 possible shapes for sprites, numbered 0 to 25. Numbers 1 to 5 are predefined, the others are initially blank. Any can be redefined using a simple shape editor to specify the pattern of dots in a 16 by 16 grid. Each of the 32 sprites can be commanded to adopt one of these 26 shapes. A neat form of animation can be obtained by commanding a sprite (or several, or all) to adopt one shape, then another, then another and so on, as it moves across the screen.

There are 96 tiles, numbered from 0 to 95. Numbers 32 to 95 initially carry the patterns of the characters engraved on the key tops – tile 33 is the exclamation mark, tile 42 is the asterisk, tiles 65 to 90 are the letters A to Z and so on. Numbers 0 to 31 are initially blank. Tiles are used when characters are to be displayed on the screen. Although any tile can be changed by using the shape editor to specify a new pattern of dots on an 8 by 8 grid, be careful: if, for instance, you change tile 72, the letter H, to be three nested squares then you will get the squares rather than the letter H in your typed commands and in error messages. It is wise to confine yourself to changing tiles 0 to 31 until you are a fairly experienced user of TI LOGO.

TI LOGO does not handle numbers with decimal parts. It only deals with integers, in the range –32767 to 32767.

C.2 Turtle Graphics, Sprites and Tiles

The screen is 254 units wide and 192 units high. The origin of co-ordinates is at the centre of the screen. When the turtle has a heading of 0 degrees it is pointing straight up the screen. The heading increases as the turtle turns clockwise. To use the turtle, give the command TELL TURTLE first.

TELL   nl

Selects what the following commands will be directed at. Examples are TELL TURTLE, TELL BACKGROUND, TELL TILE 17, TELL 3, TELL [2 7 19 30]. The command TELL 3 is the same as TELL SPRITE 3. The variable ALL has been predefined to have as its value the list consisting of the integers from 0 to 31, so you can TELL :ALL.

FORWARD (FD)   n

BACK (BK)   n

LEFT (LT)   n

RIGHT (RT)   n

DOT   n n

Puts a dot at the point whose X and Y co-ordinates are specified.

HOME

Sends the turtle or sprite(s) to the centre of the screen. No line is drawn.

CLEARSCREEN (CS)

SX   n

Sets the X co-ordinate for the turtle or sprite(s). No
line is drawn.

SY   n
Sets the Y co-ordinate for the turtle or sprite(s). No
line is drawn.

SXY   n n
Combines SX and SY.

SXV   n
Gives the sprite(s) the chosen X velocity, in the
range −127 to 127.

SYV   n
Like SXV, but Y velocity.

SV   n n
Combines SXV and SYV.

SETHEADING (SH)   n

SETSPEED (SS)   n
Gives the sprite(s) the chosen speed along the
current heading.

SETCOLOR (SC)   nl
If the input is a number, it gives the turtle pen or
sprite(s) the chosen color. Some variables have been
predefined suitably, for example SC :LIME is the same
as SC 3. The variables are CLEAR, BLACK, GREEN,
LIME, BLUE, SKY, RED, CYAN, RUST, ORANGE, YEL-
LOW, LEMON, OLIVE, PURPLE, GRAY and WHITE. How
these actually appear depends on your TV set. If it is
a tile that is being commanded, the input can be a
list of two numbers. The first selects the tile's fore-
ground, the second selects the tile's background
color.

COLORBACKGROUND (CB)
Like SETCOLOR, but affects only the screen background color.

CARRY   n
Tells the sprite(s) which shape to have. Shapes 1 to
5 are predefined, and there are appropriate predefined variables: PLANE is 1, TRUCK is 2, ROCKET is
3, BALL is 4 and BOX is 5.

MAKESHAPE (MS)   n
Invokes the shape editor to edit the chosen shape.

SHOWTURTLE (ST)

HIDETURTLE (HT)

PENDOWN (PD)

PENUP (PU)

PENERASE (PE)

PENREVERSE (PR)

NOTURTLE

    Removes the turtle and erases any turtle drawing – the reverse of TELL TURTLE.

FREEZE

    Stops all sprite motion, until the command THAW.

THAW

    Restarts all sprite motion after a FREEZE.

COLOR   => n

    Outputs the color of the turtle pen or sprite(s). If several are being commanded, the color of the first is output.

SPEED   => n

    Outputs the speed of the sprite(s). If more than one is being commanded, the speed of the first is output.

XVEL   => n

    Like SPEED: outputs the X component of the velocity.

YVEL   => n

    Like SPEED: outputs the Y component of the velocity.

WHO   => identity

    Outputs the input to the last TELL command. This may be TURTLE or TILE n, and these are neither words nor lists, but can be PRINTed.

SHAPE   => n

    Outputs the number of the shape of the sprite(s). If several are being commanded, outputs the number of the shape of the first.

XCOR   => n

    Outputs the X co-ordinate of the turtle or sprite(s).

YCOR   => n

    Outputs the Y co-ordinate of the turtle or sprite(s).

HEADING   => n

Outputs the heading of the turtle or sprite(s).

WHERE   => l

Outputs a list of three numbers, namely the turtle's co-ordinates and heading.

MAKECHAR (MC)   n

Invokes the shape editor to edit the shape on a tile.

PUTTILE (PT)   n n n

The first input is a tile number, the second is a row number (0-23) and the third is a column number (0-31). The tile is displayed there on the screen.

PRINTCHAR (PC)   n

Like PUTTILE, but prints that tile where the cursor currently is.

CHARNUM (CN)   w   => n

The input is a single character word. Outputs the number of the corresponding tile.

EACH   l

The input is a list of commands. Each commanded sprite obeys the list of commands. The procedure YOURNUMBER (YN for short) can be used in the list – each sprite recognises it as the number of itself. The list is re-evaluated for each sprite. Therefore EACH [SC RANDOM] gives each a random color, whereas SC RANDOM gives them all the same random color.

BEEP

Starts the single tone sound.

NOBEEP

Stops the sound.

WAIT   n

Waits the given number of 60ths of a second (50ths in Britain).

LOOKLIKE   n

A form of CARRY, but the input is a sprite number rather than a shape number.

C.3 Arithmetic

Numbers are integers, in the range -32767 to 32767.

+, −, *, /   n n   => n
> These are used in the conventional way. Use parentheses to avoid ambiguity.

SUM   n n   =>0 −
> SUM 3 4 outputs 7.

DIFFERENCE   n n   => n
> DIFFERENCE 7 2 outputs 5.

PRODUCT   n n   => n

QUOTIENT   n n   => n
> QUOTIENT 21 3 outputs 7.

RANDOM   => n
> Outputs a random number from 0 to 9.

C.4 Procedures

TO   w
> Input is NOT quoted.

EDIT   w
> Input is NOT quoted. It can be omitted if you have not thought of a name at the start of editing!

DEFINE   w l
> The first input is a name (it IS quoted), the second is a list of lists defining a procedure to be known by that name.

TEXT   w   => l
> Input is a name (it IS quoted). Output is a list of lists, giving the definition of the procedure named.

ERASE   w
> The input is NOT quoted. The named procedure is erased.

C.5 Words and Lists

Beware of parentheses and the minus sign inside lists. They are treated as self-contained words. The list [(−3) 4] has five elements: '(', '−', 3, ')' and 4. You must use SENTENCE if you want to include a negative number in a list, because you cannot type in the number directly as part of the list. Note also that only WORD can accept a number as input.

FIRST   wl   => nwl

LAST   wl => nwl

BUTFIRST (BF)   wl => nwl

BUTLAST (BL)   wl => nwl

SENTENCE (SE)   wl wl => l
Combines the inputs into a list. Input lists get broken into
separate elements first, as in Terrapin LOGO.

WORD   nw nw => nwl

C.6 Condition Procedures

IF t THEN ...

IF t THEN ... ELSE ...

TEST   t

IFT ...

IFF ...

>, <   n n => t
          Used in the customary way: 2 > 1, not > 2 1.

=   nwl nwl => t
          Used in the customary way: 2 = 2, not = 2 2.

GREATER   n n => t
          GREATER 5 4 is TRUE.

LESS   n n => t
          LESS 7 3 is FALSE.

IS   nwl nwl => t
          A form of '=': IS 6 3+3 is TRUE.

EITHER   t t => t

BOTH   t t => t

NOT   t => t"

C.7 Control

STOP

OUTPUT (OP)   nwl

REPEAT   n l

RUN   l
          Like REPEAT 1 ...

GO   nw

Transfers control to the line with the specified label in the same procedure. Labels are put at the start of a line, and are followed immediately (no space) by a colon.

C.8 Screen Input/Output

PRINT   nwl

TYPE   nwl

Like PRINT, but does not move on to a new line after printing.

READLINE (RL)   => l

Reads in a line typed by the user.

READCHAR (RC)   => w

Outputs a single-character word consisting of the least recent character typed but not yet read.

RC?   => t

Outputs TRUE if there are characters that have been typed but not read.

C.9 Variables

MAKE   w nwl

CALL   nwl w

MAKE with the inputs reversed.

CONTENTS   => l

Outputs a list of the names of all variables.

C.10 Information

PP

Prints the names of the procedures.

PN

Prints the names and values of all the variables.

PO   w

Prints the named procedure. The name need not be quoted.

PA

Prints all procedures, and the names and values of all variables.

C.11 Files

SAVE

Follow the instructions it gives. You can save all procedures, or all shapes and tiles, or both.

RECALL

Follow the instructions it gives.

C.12 Tracing

CONTINUE

Resumes after a pause. The key FCTN-7 is used to
cause a pause.

TRACEBACK

Used during a pause. Prints information about the
paused procedures.

C.13 Editing Keys

Any normal text you type is inserted, without overwriting existing
text. There are mnemonics above the top row of keys, or on the
front of other keys, to remind you of the function of that key
when used with FCTN. Many can be used to edit the commands
you type in directly. FCTN-R is a left square bracket. FCTN-T is
a right square bracket.

FCTN-3 (ERASE) Erases the character to the left of the cursor. If
at the start of a line, joins the line to the previous one.

FCTN-1 (DELETE) Erases the character where the cursor is. If it
is at the end of a line, joins the line to the next one.

FCTN-5 (BEGIN) Moves the cursor to the start of the current
LOGO line.

FCTN-6 (PROC'D) Moves the cursor to the end of the current
LOGO line.

FCTN-4 (CLEAR) Erases from the cursor to the end of the current
LOGO line.

FCTN-E (up-arrow) Moves the cursor up a line.

FCTN-X (down-arrow) Moves the cursor down a line.

FCTN-S (left-arrow) Moves the cursor left one character.

FCTN-D (right-arrow) Moves the cursor right one character.

FCTN-9 (BACK) Ends editing. Also used to abort the running of a procedure.

C.14 Shape editing

You see a grid of squares. The cursor is a flashing square filling one of the grid squares. The keys E (up), X (down), S (left) and D (right) move the cursor one square, leaving the square it was on empty. Using these keys with FCTN also moves the cursor, but leaves the square it was on full. FCTN-9 (BACK) ends the editing.

C.15 Special Commands

FCTN-= exits TI LOGO. The command BYE does the same.

Appendix D
Radio Shack Color LOGO

D.1 RADIO SHACK COLOR LOGO

Radio Shack Color LOGO is a product of Micropi, and is licensed to Tandy Corporation. It is very different from the other versions of LOGO that have been described. There is no provision for working with lists or with words, only integers. It is essentially a turtle graphics system, but with some powerful features beyond those described in the main text of this book (which is why this appendix is included).

The most outstanding feature of the system is that you can have many turtles, each obeying its own LOGO procedure, on the screen at once. Because of the nature of the computer hardware, the turtles do not literally all move 'at once'; each gets to move a little in turn. Provided that you do not have too many turtles on the screen, the computer works fast enough to give you the impression of simultaneous movement. If you do have lots of turtles, you will be able to see a 'rippling' effect produced by the small but perceptible hesitation in each turtle's motion. Turtles can send messages to each other. A message, however, is just an integer; if you want a turtle to send more complicated information, such as its co-ordinates, then you must have it send a sequence of messages.

The way Radio Shack Color LOGO is used is also markedly different to the other LOGO systems. There are four 'modes' of interaction: BREAK mode, RUN mode, EDIT mode and DOODLE mode. When you first start this LOGO, you cannot immediately give LOGO commands, because you are in BREAK mode. BREAK mode has three purposes: to give access to the EDIT and the RUN modes, to let you load or save programs using disk or cassette and to let you make a copy of LOGO procedures on a printer.

EDIT mode lets you edit LOGO procedures. You do not edit a single procedure; instead, you always get access to all the existing procedures, so that you can change one or several, or add or delete procedures as you wish, in one piece of editing.

As the name suggests, RUN mode is the mode to select when you want to give commands. Unfortunately, the rules about commands in RUN mode are not the same as those for commands within procedures. The differences are that some commands are not possible in RUN mode, and only one command is allowed per line. In the summary below, the commands that are NOT usable in RUN mode are noted.

DOODLE mode lets very young users construct simple drawings. In this mode, the numeric keys each do a simple turtle command, such as FORWARD 10 or LEFT 45.

To get from BREAK mode to RUN mode, press 'R'.
To get from BREAK mode to EDIT mode, press 'E'.
To get to DOODLE mode, get into RUN mode and press '@'.
To return to BREAK mode, press the BREAK key.

D.2 Conventions

The conventions are the same as those explained at the start of Appendix A.

D.3 Turtle Graphics

The origin of co-ordinates is at the bottom left of the screen. The screen is 256 units wide (0 to 255) and 192 units high (0 to 191). The turtle starts in the centre of the screen. Its initial heading is 0, straight upward. The turtle turns clockwise as its heading increases.

The turtle can only be precisely at a point with integer co-ordinates, not part of the way between two such points. Because of this, the command

    REPEAT 360 [FD 1 RT 1]

draws an octagon rather than a circle. For the first 22 repetitions, the turtle goes to the next point vertically upward. At the 23rd, the heading is such that the nearest point for the turtle to go to is the one up and to the left, and this is the start of the second side of the octagon. Therefore the point to bear in mind is: do not combine small turtle movements with small changes in direction. The command

    REPEAT 36 [FD 10 RT 10]

draws a very reasonable circle (and very quickly).

There is one master turtle, and up to 254 other turtles. Each turtle is identified by an integer, specified at the time it is brought into existence ('hatched'). The identifying integer must be in the range 1 to 254 – the master turtle is turtle 0. Many turtles can have the same identifying integer. When more than just one turtle is being used, each turtle in turn obeys one basic command. This includes the master turtle, so the master turtle must have at least as much to do as every other one, otherwise the system will make all the others wait each time until you give a further command to the master turtle. This is awkward but there is a simple device to spare you too much convoluted forethought: you can make the master turtle (or any other) vanish, in which case it no longer needs to get a turn. The master turtle reappears if there are no other turtles around, or if there are no unfinished procedures. Other turtles never reappear except by being 'hatched' again.

FORWARD (FD)   n

BACK (BK)   n

RIGHT (RT)   n

LEFT (LT)   n

HOME

CLEAR
    Wipes off any drawing and sends the commanded turtle to the home position.

PENDOWN (PD)

PENUP (PU)

PENCOLOR (PC)   n
    Colours are 0, 1, 2 and 3. The default is 0. The actual color depends on your TV set.

BACKGROUND (BG)   n
    Like PENCOLOR, but sets the background color. Erasing is done by drawing in the background color.

COLORSET   n
    The input must be 0 or 1. There are two possible sets of the four colors 0-3, and this command selects the one to use. The default is 0.

HATCH   n procedure & arguments

Hatches a turtle, which has the same position and heading as the parent turtle at that moment. The first input is the identifying number for the child turtle (this is used when sending and receiving messages). The rest of the input line is the name of the procedure, together with any needed inputs, that the hatched turtle is to obey. When the procedure ends, if ever, the hatched turtle vanishes.

VANISH

Makes the commanded turtle go out of existence. If it is the master turtle, it will reappear if no other turtles are left with anything to do.

SETX (SX)   n

SETY (SY)   n

SETHEADING (SH)   n

SHOWTURTLE (ST)

HIDETURTLE (HT)

SHAPE   definition

The input is a sequence of letters: F, B, L, R, U and D for forward one dot, back one dot, left 45, right 45, put the shape pen up and put the shape pen down. If the sequence is too long to fit on one line, a minus sign can be used to indicate that the sequence continues on the next line. The shape pen is only for redefining how the turtle looks on the screen. It is not the same as the turtle's pen. Can only be used in a procedure.

WRAP

When wrapping, no part of a line that crosses the edge of the screen ever gets drawn.

NOWRAP

SLOW   n

Sets the speed of motion of all turtles at once. The input must be in the range 0 (fastest) to 127 (slowest).

XLOC   n => n

Gives the X co-ordinate of the turtle identified by the input number. If there is more than one such turtle, one is selected and its X co-ordinate is output. The input must be enclosed in parentheses if it is an expression.

YLOC   n   => n

Like XLOC, but outputs the Y co-ordinate. The input must be enclosed in parentheses if it is an expression.

HEADING   n   => n

Like XLOC, but outputs the heading. The input must be enclosed in parentheses if it is an expression.

ME   => n

Outputs the identifying number of the commanded turtle.

NEAR   n   => n

The input is the identifying number of some turtle(s). Outputs the sum of the horizontal and vertical distances between the commanded turtle and one turtle having the given identifying number. If there is no such turtle, then the measuring point used is the home position. The input must be enclosed in parentheses if it is an expression.

SEND   n n

Sends the message (just an integer) specified by the second input, to the turtle identified by the first input. If there is more than one such turtle, the first one to look at its mail gets the message. An identifier of 255 means that the message is for any turtle; the first to read its mail gets the message. The input must be enclosed in parentheses if it is an expression.

MAIL   n   => n

The input is the identifying number of the turtle from which a message is to be read. An identifier of 255 means that a message from any turtle is to be read. The oldest unread message is output, or 0 is output if there is no message to be read. The input must be enclosed in parentheses if it is an expression.

D.4 Arithmetic

Radio Shack Color LOGO only deals with integers, in the range -32768 to 32767. The numeric code corresponding to a key can be entered as a single quote followed by the key – for instance, 'A is the same as 65.

+, −, *, /		n n => n	

These are used in the conventional way: 2 + 3, not + 2 3.

ABS   n => n

Outputs the input with the sign changed, if necessary, to make it non-negative. The input must be enclosed in parentheses if it is an expression.

RANDOM   n

Outputs a random integer in the range 0 to one less than the input. The input must be enclosed in parentheses if it is an expression.

D.5 Procedures

You must switch to EDIT mode (press BREAK, then E). You get access to all procedure definitions, so you can add more and delete or change any existing ones in a single editing session. When you add new definitions, the first line must begin with the word TO (and there must be no space before it). The TO is followed by the name of the procedure (no quote), and then up to five input names, each beginning with a colon as in Terrapin LOGO. The end of one definition is denoted by the word END, also as in Terrapin LOGO.

D.6 Condition Procedures

The words TRUE and FALSE are not used in Radio Shack Color LOGO. Instead, the number 0 denotes 'false' and any non-zero number denotes 'true'. Logical tests that work out true always output 1.

>, <, =   n n => n

Used in the conventional way.

>=, <=, <>   n n => n

Used in the conventional way. The '<>' means 'not equal to'.

&   n n => n

Used as 'and', and comes in between the inputs. Ouputs 1 only if both the inputs are non-zero, otherwise outputs 0.

!   n n => n

Used as 'or', and comes in between the inputs.

Outputs 1 if either input is non-zero, otherwise outputs 0.

NOT   n => n

Outputs 1 if the input is zero, otherwise outputs 0.

D.7 Control

IF n (commands)   —

Note that THEN is not used, and that the commands must be enclosed in parentheses. The commands are obeyed if the first input is non-zero. Can only be used inside a procedure.

IF n (commands) ELSE (commands)

Can only be used inside a procedure.

REPEAT   n (commands)

Note that the commands are enclosed in parentheses. Can only be used inside a procedure.

WHILE   n (commands)

The first input is evaluated. If it is non-zero, the commands are obeyed. The first input is re-evaluated, and the commands re-obeyed, until the first input works out to be 0. Thus WHILE 1 (...) is a simple way of making something happen forever, or until interrupted, whichever is the sooner. To interrupt use BREAK – this also selects BREAK mode. Can only be used inside a procedure.

STOP

Can only be used inside a procedure.

D.8 Input/Output

To save or load procedures on cassette or disk, you must enter BREAK mode (press the BREAK key) – see the manual for details.

PRINT   n

PRINT   string

You can print a string of characters by surrounding them with double quote marks – for instance, PRINT "HELLO WORLD". The printing appears starting at the location of the commanded turtle.

KEY   => n

Outputs the numeric code corresponding to the key currently being pressed, or 0 if no key is being pressed.

PADDLE $n \Rightarrow n$

The input is an integer in the range 0 to 3. The input 0 refers to the up/down displacement of the left paddle, the input 1 refers to the left/right displacement of the left paddle, and 2 and 3 refer similarly to the right paddle. The output is a measure of the displacement, in the range 0 to 63. Fully up or fully left is 0. The input must be enclosed in parentheses if it is an expression.

D.9 Editing Keys

The only line you get a chance to alter is the one at the bottom of the screen. Pressing SHIFT CLEAR in BREAK mode wipes out all definitions. To enter EDIT mode, press BREAK to get into BREAK mode, then press E. Normally, what you type overwrites whatever is on the same line. You can insert one of the special key command codes by typing an asterisk first. To type in an asterisk you must type two asterisks.

ENTER   Moves the text up one line. If you are at the end of all text, adds a new line.

→   Moves the cursor right one character. If used with SHIFT, inserts a blank space into the line by moving the right-hand part rightward, provided there is space left on the line.

←   Moves the cursor left one character. If used with SHIFT, deletes the character where the cursor is and closes the gap. If the line is empty, it is removed.

UP-ARROW   Moves the text up one line. If used with SHIFT, starts the text moving up automatically until any key is pressed.

DOWN-ARROW   Moves the text down one line. If used with SHIFT, inserts a complete lineful of spaces where the cursor is.

CLEAR   Moves the cursor to the top of all the text.

D.10 DOODLE Mode

To enter DOODLE mode, enter RUN mode then press '@'. The next line you type will be taken as the name of a procedure. Thereafter, the numeric keys can be used to provide some simple LOGO commands – see the manual for details – and the commands are automatically added to the definition of the procedure. To exit DOODLE mode, and thereby end the procedure defining as well, press BREAK. This returns you to BREAK mode.

D.11 An Example

The program in this section is a 'minefield' type game. The object is to manoeuvre one 'roving' turtle from bottom left to top right, using small steps controlled by the 'F', 'B', 'L' and 'R' keys. There are a dozen invisible turtles randomly spread around, with two at edges to thwart the obvious algorithm; they do nothing but test for the approach of the 'roving' one. If it comes fairly near (less than 40) a sentry, the sentry sends a message to the rover, which blinks twice thus giving the user warning of nearby danger. If it comes too near, the sentry explodes (in fairly slow motion) and sends a different message to the rover which is then forced to return to bottom left; the sentry clears the screen, so you have to remember your path and where you got warnings. The top right of the screen has a turtle in the 'base' watching for the rover coming. If it gets there, the 'base' draws a fence, to indicate success, and sends a message to the rover to return it to the start so the game can start over. Lots of refinements are possible, such as having a scorer, having a supply of rocks so that the rover can lob some around to try to explode mines safely, and so on.

  The procedure WATCH is what each sentry does. The initial WAIT 50 makes sure that no sentry sends any messages during the setting up stage – WAIT is defined below. The roving turtle has identity number 100.

```
TO WATCH
  HT
  WAIT 50
  WHILE 1
  (IF NEAR 100 < 40
      (SEND 100 1 WAIT 15 )
    IF NEAR 100 < 20
      (BANG SEND 100 2 WAIT 15 )
```

```
    )
   END
```

The procedure WAIT is for wasting time.

```
   TO WAIT :D
    REPEAT :D ()
   END
```

The procedure BANG draws a little explosion.

```
   TO BANG
    REPEAT 12
       (RT 33 FD 20 LT 3 BK 20)
   END
```

The procedure SEEK is what the roving turtle does. The WHILE 1 (...) loop awaits a key press by the user, and makes the rover move appropriately. After each move, the rover looks to see if any turtle has sent it mail. If the message is 1, the rover blinks twice, warning the user that it is near an invisible sentry. If the message is 2, the rover causes the screen to clear, and it leaps back to the start. The message 2 only gets sent by a sentry if the rover is too close, and the sentry has already done the procedure BANG, drawing an explosion.

```
   TO SEEK
    WHILE 1
    (MAKE :K KEY
      IF :K
        (IF :K='F (FD 10)
          IF :K='B (BK 10)
          IF :K='R (RT 45)
          IF :K='L (LT 45)
        )
     MAKE :M MAIL 255
     IF :M
       (IF :M=1 (HT ST HT ST)
        ELSE (CLEAR SX 5 SY 5)
        )
     )
   END
```

The base turtle, that the rover is trying to reach, obeys the procedure BASE. It repeatedly looks to see if the rover is close. If so, it draws a fence, to tell the user that he has won, then sends the rover the message 2, and the rover clears the screen and returns to the start.

```
   TO BASE
```

```
WHILE 1
(IF NEAR 100 < 30
    (SH 180 SX 225 SY 192
     FD 30 LT 90 FD 30
     SX 245 SY 180
     WAIT 100
     SEND 100 2
     WAIT 25)
 )
END
```

The main procedure is PLAY, it starts everything else. The first REPEAT command creates the first ten sentries, moving the master turtle to some random spot that is not too near the start and not too near the finish. The next four lines create two more randomly placed sentries, one of which is somewhere on the left-hand edge of the screen and the other of which is somewhere along the bottom edge. These two are specially placed to prevent the user from moving the rover along the outside edge of the screen; otherwise this would be a comparatively easy ploy. The next two lines place the base turtle at the finish (X=245, Y=180), and start it looking for the arrival of the rover. Then the rover itself is created at the start position (X=5, Y=5) and it starts to obey the procedure SEEK defined above. The final VANISH command gets rid of the master turtle, so that the sentries, the base and the rover turtles do not need to wait for the master turtle to have a turn.

```
TO PLAY
REPEAT 10
    (SX 30 + RANDOM 196
     SY 30 + RANDOM 132
     HATCH 1 WATCH)
SX 5 SY 30 + RANDOM 132
HATCH 1 WATCH
SY 5 SX 30 + RANDOM 196
HATCH 1 WATCH
SX 245 SY 180
HATCH 1 BASE
SX 5 SY 5
HATCH 100 SEEK
VANISH
END
```

Appendix E
Research Machines LOGO

E.1 Research Machines LOGO

Research Machines LOGO is distributed by

> Research Machines Ltd.,
> P.O. Box 75,
> Oxford OX2 0BW
> England

It is designed to run under the CP/M operating system, on Research Machines microcomputers. At present it runs on two types of Z80-based machines. These have special graphics hardware, so this LOGO will not run on other Z80-based CP/M systems.

Research Machines LOGO is a dialect of LOGO designed at the Department of Artificial Intelligence of the University of Edinburgh. Many of the procedure names are different to those used in versions such as Terrapin LOGO that are based on the M.I.T. dialect. The facilities it offers are broadly similar to those of Terrapin LOGO.

E.2 Conventions

The description uses the notation described in section A.1. The differences from Terrapin LOGO are pointed out in the notes that follow. A crucial difference is that Research Machines LOGO uses a single quote (apostrophe) rather than the double quote mark, for differentiating between words and procedures.

E.3 Turtle Graphics

The screen is 320 units wide by 192 unit high. The origin of co-ordinates is at the bottom left of the screen; the turtle initially starts at X=160, Y=95 in the middle of the screen. When the turtle has a heading of 0 degrees it is pointing rightward. Unlike other LOGO systems, the heading increases as the turtle turns anticlockwise. There is no equivalent of WRAP or TURTLESTATE. Terrapin LOGO has no equivalent of SLOW, LABEL or NOEDGES.

FORWARD (FD)   n

BACKWARD (BD)   n
                Note, the abbreviation is not BK.

LEFT (LT)   n

RIGHT (RT)   n

CLEAN (CL)
                Terrapin LOGO CLEARSCREEN. Clears the drawing, does not affect the turtle.

CENTRE (CT)
                Returns the turtle to its initial position. Does not draw a line, under any circumstances. Can also be spelt CENTER.

EDGES
                After this command, the turtle is not allowed to cross the edge of the screen. This is the default circumstance.

NOEDGES
                After this command, the turtle can cross the edge of the screen, though it does not wrap. The turtle's co-ordinates are limited to the range −32757 to +32757.

SLOW
                Selects the slower of the two turtle speeds. This is the default.

FAST
                Selects the faster of the two speeds, which is comparable to the speed in Terrapin LOGO.

SETX   n
                Does not draw a line.

SETY   n
                Does not draw a line.

SETH   n

ARCL   n n

Draws an arc bending leftwards. The first input is the radius, the second is the angle.

ARCR   n n

Like ARCL, but draws an arc bending rightwards.

LABEL   nwl

Prints its input as part of the drawing, starting at the turtle's position. The turtle's state is not changed.

PENCIL   n

The input must be in the range 0–3. Pencil 0 is the same as Terrapin LOGO PENUP. The other three are red, green and blue. This command is a combination of Terrapin LOGO PC and PD or PU.

ERASER

Makes the turtle erase as it moves. Can also be spelt RUBBER.

LIFT

Terrapin LOGO PENUP.

REVEAL

Terrapin LOGO SHOWTURTLE.

HIDE

Terrapin LOGO HIDETURTLE.

WHERE   => l

Outputs a list of three numbers. The first two are the turtle's X and Y co-ordinates and the third is its heading.

DRAWING

Restricts text such as typed commands to the bottom four lines of the screen, so that text does not obscure the drawing.

TEXT

Renders the drawing invisible, so that the drawing does not obscure text. MIX, DRAWING or any turtle command makes the drawing visible.

MIX

Allows both text and drawing to use the full screen, though the drawing area does not extend to the bottom four lines on the screen.

PICTURE

Sends a copy of the drawing to the printer. The system can be told of the printer type in several ways;

if the system does not know it, it will ask you.

E.4 Arithmetic

Numbers can be given either as integers or as numbers with a decimal part, such as:

    -317
    67.891

There is no exponent notation. Numbers are only accurate to seven significant figures, though they can have up to 38 digits on either side of the decimal point. Another important difference is that Research Machines LOGO does not use the conventional +, -, * and / for arithmetic. Instead, the procedures ADD, SUB, MUL and DIV are used.

ADD   n n   => n

SUBTRACT (SUB)   n n   => n

MULTIPLY (MUL)   n n   => n

DIVIDE (DIV)   n n   => n

SHARE   n n   => n
               Like DIVIDE, but the output is the integer part of the division.

DECIMALS   n
               The input must be an integer from 0 to 6. This determines the number of decimal places to be used when printing numbers. An important point is that in this LOGO, numbers which look equal when printed are equal, and those which look unequal are unequal.

SIN   n   => n

COS   n   => n

TAN   n   => n

SQT   n   => n

REMAINDER (REM)   n   => n
               Outputs remainder when the first input is divided by the

PICK   n   => n
               Outputs a random integer between 1 and its input.

RANDOM   => n

Outputs a random number between 0 and 0.999999.

E.5 Procedures

There is no equivalent of the Terrapin LOGO DEFINE and TEXT. Terrapin LOGO has no equivalent of INSPECT or RESTORE.

BUILD   w

Terrapin LOGO TO. The input can be quoted or unquoted.

CHANGE   w

Like Terrapin LOGO EDIT, but the named procedure must exist. The input can be quoted or unquoted.

INSPECT   w

Like CHANGE, but it does not allow you to change the procedure. No backup copy is made either. The input can be quoted or unquoted.

RESTORE

Undoes what the last CHANGE did.

SCRAP   wl

Like Terrapin LOGO ERASE. Deletes the named procedure(s).

COPY   wl

Sends a copy of the named procedure(s) to the printer.

E.6 Words and Lists

There is no empty word. Research Machines LOGO has two very useful features. The first is 'dynamic lists', akin to Terrapin LOGO SENTENCE. They are like ordinary lists, but angle brackets are used instead of square brackets. The contents of the list is a sequence of expressions. When the command containing the dynamic list is obeyed, the expressions are evaluated and the outputs formed into a list. For example,

    PRINT <FIRST [TAKE OFF] ADD 2 3>

prints [TAKE 5].

The other feature is list subscripting. A hash sign ('#') introduces a subscript. The following is an example:

    MAKE 'X [THIS IS A LIST]

PRINT :X # 4

prints LIST, and

MAKE 'X # 1 :X
PRINT :X

prints [[THIS IS A LIST] IS A LIST]. Subscripts can be compounded:

PRINT :X # 1 # 1

now prints THIS. This must be used if you want a counterpart of the Terrapin LOGO LAST. The Terrapin LOGO expression

LAST :X

would be

:X # COUNT :X

FIRST   wl => nwl
                Does not accept a number as input.

REST   wl => wl
                Terrapin LOGO BUTFIRST.

JOIN   wl wl => wl
                Joins two words or lists into one.

PUTFIRST (PF)   nwl l => l
                Puts the first input onto the front of the list given as
                second input, and outputs the resulting list.

PUTLAST (PL)   l nwl => l
                Somewhat like PUTFIRST. Note that the inputs are
                switched round.

COUNT   nwl => n
                Outputs the number of elements or characters in the
                input. If the input is a number, the output is the
                number of digits to the left of the decimal point, at
                least 1.

E.7 Condition Procedures

Procedures that test some condition usually have names ending in 'Q', rather than '?' as in Terrapin LOGO. Research Machines LOGO also uses procedures such as EQUALQ rather than '='.

IF t THEN ...

IF t THEN ... ELSE ...

> You can also have expressions rather than commands after the THEN and ELSE, in which case the whole IF ... outputs a result.

EQUALQ (EQQ)   nwl nwl => t

GREATERQ (GRQ)   nw nw => t

GREATEREQUALQ (GEQ)   nw nw => t

LESSQ (LSQ)   nw nw => t

LESSEQUALQ (LEQ)   nw nw => t

NUMBERQ (NQ)   nwl => t

WORDQ (WQ)   nwl => t

LISTQ (LQ)   nwl => t

ZEROQ (ZQ)   nwl => t

EMPTYQ (EMQ)   l => t

KEYQ   => t

> Outputs TRUE if a key has been pressed but not yet read in by LOGO.

BOTH   t t => t

EITHER   t t => t

XOR   t t => t

> Outputs TRUE if one input is TRUE and the other FALSE.

NOT   t => t

E.8 Control

Research Machines LOGO has a DO and a WHILE command as well as REPEAT. The REPEAT command does not expect the commands in a list. By default, it repeats all the commands from the REPEAT to the end of the line, although you can change this by using parentheses to enclose the REPEAT and all the commands it is to repeat.

STOP

ESCAPE

> Terrapin LOGO TOPLEVEL.

RESULT   nwl
                Terrapin LOGO OUTPUT.

REPEAT   n commands

DO commands UNTIL t

WHILE   t commands

RUN   w inputs
                Runs the command named by the first input. Any
                necessary inputs for the command must follow.

PAUSE   n
                Waits the given number of complete seconds.

E.9 Screen Input/Output

There is no counterpart of the Terrapin LOGO procedures ASCII,
CHAR, CURSOR or the paddles. It is possible to simulate CURSOR
and PRINT1 by using LABEL (see section E.3).

PRINT   nwl
                Lists are printed with the outermost square brackets.

SAY   nwl
                Like PRINT, but lists are printed without the outermost
                square brackets.

ASK   l => l
                Prints the input, without the outermost bracket, and
                appends a question mark. Waits for the user to type
                a line in reply, then outputs that line as a list. Simi-
                lar to Terrapin LOGO REQUEST.

KEY   => w
                Outputs a single-character word consisting of the
                least recent key pressed but not yet read in.

E.10 Variables

MAKE   w nwl
                If the variable already exists and has a list as its
                value, you can use the subscripting mechanism
                explained in section E.6 to change the value of one
                element.

VALUE (:)   w => nwl
                Like Terrapin LOGO THING. If the value is a list, you

can use the subscripting mechanism explained in section E.6 to select one element.

NEW   w

Creates a new variable which supercedes any other of the same name until the procedure in which it is used ends. Initially the new temporary variable has no value.

E.11 Information

FILES

Terrapin LOGO CATALOG.

PROCEDURES

Prints out the names of the user-defined procedures.

INDEX

Prints the names of the procedures in the active file.

E.12 Files

There is no way to save pictures, though they can be printed.

KEEP   wl

Keeps the named procedure(s) in the active file.

GET   wl

Gets the named procedure(s) from the active file.

LOSE   wl

Deletes the named procedure(s) from the active file.

FILENAME   w

Selects the named file as the active one.

DISK   w

The input is a single-character word. Selects that disk as the active one.

INITIALISE

Resets the active disk and file to the default. This is necessary if you change disks, otherwise CP/M loses track of the disks.

E.13 Tracing

Research Machines LOGO has some very powerful features.

TERSE

> Selects a short form for the error messages.

VERBOSE

> Selects the normal, detailed form of error messages.

TRACE **wl**

> Marks the named procedure(s) for tracing. When run, LOGO will report the fact, report the values of the inputs and of any output.

UNTRACE **wl**

WALK **wl**

> Marks the named procedure(s) for walking. When run, LOGO will expect a response from you before obeying each line. The RETURN key means 'do that line', CTRL-C means 'do not bother to ask for other lines in this procedure'. CTRL-F means 'do no more asking'.

UNWALK **wl**

BUG **wl**

> Marks the named variable(s) for tracing. LOGO will report the new value whenever the value is changed.

UNBUG **wl**

E.14 Editing Keys

The model used is different from that of Terrapin LOGO. The cursor can move to anywhere in the window, not just within the text of the procedure. Only one procedure can be edited at once. Normal typing is inserted where the cursor is, without overwriting existing text. The editor arranges that a word is never broken in two by overlapping the right-hand edge of the screen.

CTRL-L Cursor left.

CTRL-R Cursor right.

CTRL-U Cursor up.

CTRL-D Cursor down.

DEL Deletes the character to the left of the cursor and closes up the gap.

CTRL-X Deletes the character the cursor is standing on, and closes the gap.

RETURN Moves the cursor to the start of the next line.

CTRL-S Inserts a lineful of spaces.

CTRL-K Deletes the line on which the cursor is standing.

CTRL-B Moves the cursor to the beginning of the procedure.

CTRL-E Moves the cursor to the end of the procedure.

CTRL-C Moves the cursor to the top left corner of the window.

CTRL-G Moves the cursor up 8 lines, moving the text if necessary.

CTRL-T Moves the cursor down 8 lines, moving the cursor if necessary.

CTRL-H Displays part of the 'help' text describing the editing keys.

ESCAPE Ends the editing session.

CTRL-Z Aborts the editing session.

E.15 Other Special Keys

ESCAPE Interrupts any command and returns LOGO to waiting for the next command.

CTRL-Z Interrupts any command, like ESCAPE, but also prints useful information: the names of the procedures in progress, in reverse chronological order, the names and values of their inputs, and the name and value of any variable created by a NEW command, and the names and values of all other variables. The printing of all this can be interrupted by ESCAPE or another CTRL-Z.

E.16 Special Commands

GOODBYE
        Exits gracefully from LOGO, returns you to CP/M.

Appendix F
Answers

Chapter 2

(1)   It depends. Normally the turtle just reappears at the opposite edge. You can change this by the Terrapin LOGO command NOWRAP; thereafter, attempting to cross the edge will produce the error message

TURTLE OUT OF BOUNDS

To revert to normal, use the command WRAP. In Apple LOGO, the procedure NOWRAP does not exist by that name, but is called FENCE instead. Apple LOGO also has WINDOW, which allows the turtle to wander off the screen but doesn't make it reappear at the opposite edge. Instead, it makes the screen into a window onto the centre of a huge flat drawing area. Other LOGOs have other possibilities.

(2)   In Terrapin LOGO and Apple LOGO the screen is 280 wide and 240 high. From the initial position of the turtle, it is 120.625 to the top edge, 119.375 to the bottom edge, 140.5 to the left edge and 139.5 to the right edge. Yes, this means that the turtle does not start exactly in the middle of the screen.

(3)   To be dreadfully precise:

49.115 degrees for the top right corner,
130.51 degrees for the bottom right corner,
229.647 degrees for the bottom left corner,
310.648 degrees for the top left corner.

For nearly all purposes, the answers 49, 131, 230 and 311 are good enough.

235

(4)   Yes. FD -100 is BK 100, LT -53 is RT 53 and so on.

(5)   Yes, they do. Try the command FD 0.3 ten times, and you will get a line 3 units long. The command FD 0.003 one thousand times will do the same thing. The way to test this without old age catching up on you is in chapter 2 – the REPEAT command. LT and RT also happily work with numbers with decimal parts.

(6a)   For a pentagon the angle is 72 degrees. For a hexagon the angle is 60 degrees. For a 7-sided polygon the angle is 51.429 degrees.

(6b)   This is up to you.

(7)   The rules about layout of commands are a mess. There are two worth remembering explicitly: if one space is necessary at some point, then it is acceptable to have more, and it is wise to put a space before a right parenthesis.

(8)   This is up to you.

(9)   As you might hope, they work. For example, 3 - -4 is 7.

(10)   Dividing by zero produces the message

        CAN'T DIVIDE BY ZERO

        Too large or too minute a result is signalled by

        NUMBER TOO LARGE OR TOO SMALL IN operation

(11)   Let the increment be N. If N is a multiple of 8 there will be infinitely many blobs. Otherwise there will be

        1 + N/(highest common factor of 360 and N)

        Why is there an exception when N is a multiple of 8, you may ask? Because that is the only time when the highest common factor of N and 180 is not the same as the highest common factor of N and 360. If N is not a multiple of 8, the turtle will at some point reach an effective heading of 180 degrees, and start retracing its steps, BEFORE it reaches an exact multiple of 360 degrees and starts to repeat the figure from its new position.

(12) You can get some fancy spirals, at the very least.

(13) If 'two-dimensional random walk' means that at each step there are just four choices of direction (up, down, left, right) then the answer is yes, it definitely returns to the start eventually. If there are more choices, the situation is much more complicated, but the short answer is 'probably'.

(14) It all depends. Have a look at 'An Introduction to Probability Theory' by William Feller, 2 vols, pub. by Random House, if you really want to get into this and you are good at mathematics.

(15) In a one-dimensional walk the turtle definitely returns to the start. Try making the step size depend on direction.

Chapter 3

(1) Yes. Change the inputs to ANIMATE a little each time – make the last line of the definition something like this:

```
ANIMATE :X * 1.1 :Y * 1.2
```

(2) Yes. Give SQUARE an input, to be the side of the square, like this:

```
TO SQUARE :S
SETX XCOR + :S
SETY YCOR + :S
SETX XCOR - :S
SETY YCOR - :S
END

TO ANIMATE :X :Y :S
PC 1 SQUARE :S
PC 0 SQUARE :S
PU SETXY XCOR + :X YCOR + :Y PD
ANIMATE :X :Y :S + 0.5
END
```

The effect gets less realistic as the side of the square gets bigger.

(3) Not really. You can have LOGO do the necessary trigonometric calculations, or revert to drawing a square by

using FD and RT, but either way is significantly slower than the square used in the chapter.

(4)   It doesn't, though you may think otherwise.

(5)   Basic method A is very poor, because CS takes a fairly long time to finish. It makes the gap between each 'frame' much too long to give the illusion of animation.

(6)   Yes. Instead of REPEAT 61000 [], make the last line of TICK

          PC 6 REPEAT 60 [SEC]

where SEC is defined as

          TO SEC
          SETH :SECOND FD 30
          REPEAT 750 []
          BK 30
          MAKE "SECOND :SECOND + 6
          END

You will need to initialise SECOND to be 0 before staring the clock. The delay of REPEAT 750 [] may need to be tuned somewhat. Pen color 6 is used because you cannot really afford to have a hiccup once a minute to redraw the hour and minute hands if the seconds hand erases them. This is acceptable when there is no seconds hand, because both hands get redrawn every minute; with a seconds hand it would mean redrawing all three once a second, or a much fancier version of TICK.

(7)   This is left for you.

(8)   The procedure definition is up to you. It is surprising how hard it is to get used to a backward-running clock at first, and how natural it eventually becomes.

(9)   It does nothing. The condition is FALSE.

(10)   It prints OK, because −12 < 5.

(11)   It prints FALSE.

(12)   It prints FALSE. The condition is −11.3333 = 7.

(13)   It is a trick question. You would get the error message

         IF DOESN'T LIKE −12 AS INPUT. IT EXPECTS
         TRUE OR FALSE

(14)   You get the message

         NO STORAGE LEFT!, IN LINE
          IF :N = 1 THEN OUTPUT 1 ELSE OUTPUT
          :N * FACTORIAL :N − 1
         OF FACTORIAL, AT LEVEL something

         because the stopping condition never holds and recursion
         continues till there is no more space left for LOGO to
         keep track of what's happening. Once the message
         appears, LOGO reclaims a lot of temporarily used space,
         so don't panic, nothing awful has happened.

(15)   It can be used, for numbers larger than 1, but it is not
         particularly sensible, because there is a much more con-
         venient answer. Use SQRT SQRT :N instead!

(16)   For numbers between 0 and 1, you need to reverse the
         test

             :AV * :AV * :AV > :N

         You can change CUBE.ROOT so that it checks whether :N
         lies between 0 and 1, and does the appropriate test.   For
         negative numbers, change CU.RT:

         TO CU.RT :N
         IF :N<0 THEN OUTPUT −CUBE.ROOT −:N 1
             (−:N) ELSE OUTPUT CUBE.ROOT :N 1 :N
         END

(17)   There is a problem caused by the limited accuracy of
         numbers. Suppose :LOW is 1.70994, and :HIGH is 1.70995.
         Then LOGO will calculate the value of AV as 1.70994.
         However, if it is the cube root of 5 that is being sought,
         the cube of 1.70994 is only 4.99986, so CUBE.ROOT will
         recurse. The new inputs will be 5, 1.70994 and 1.70995 −
         which are the same as before. The recursion will not stop
         until the available space for keeping track of recursion
         gets used up.

(18)   It is very like the cube root example:

```
TO ARCSIN :VAL
OUTPUT ASIN :VAL (-90) 90
END

TO ASIN :V :L :H
MAKE "AV (:L + :H ) / 2
IF ANYOF :AV = :L :AV = :H THEN OUTPUT
     :AV
IF SIN :AV < :V THEN OUTPUT ASIN :V :AV
        :H ELSE OUTPUT ASIN :V :L :AV
END
```

Chapter 4

(1)   One of many answers:

```
TO REVERSE :L
IF :L = [] THEN OUTPUT []
OUTPUT LPUT FIRST :L REVERSE BF :L
END
```

(2)   One of many answers:

```
TO REVWORD :W
IF :W = " THEN OUTPUT "
OUTPUT WORD REVWORD BF :W FIRST :W
END
```

(3)   One of many answers:

```
TO PALINDROME :X
IF COUNT :X < 2 THEN OUTPUT "TRUE
IF (FIRST :X ) = (LAST :X ) THEN OUTPUT
        PALINDROME BF BL :X ELSE OUTPUT
        "FALSE
END
```

This uses the version of COUNT that works both for lists
and for words.

(4)   A procedure that prints out a list in the way suggested in
the exercise would be

```
TO LIST.PRINT :L
LPRINT :L 0
END
```

```
TO LPRINT :L :INDENT
IF :L = [] THEN STOP
IF LIST? FIRST :L THEN LPRINT FIRST :L
      :INDENT + 4 ELSE REPEAT :INDENT
      [PRINT1 "' '] PRINT FIRST :L
LPRINT BF :L :INDENT
END
```

Chapter 5

(1)   Sorry – it IS false. The truth is that the nested polygons
        do get somewhat 'more regular', but they also tend to get
        more like the second one back in the sequence; there are
        really two interleaved sequences of hexagons. Within either
        sequence, opposite sides tend to become parallel, and to
        lie parallel to the corresponding diagonals. An interesting
        detail is that the two sequences both 'converge' on the
        same point, and that point is the 'centre of mass' of
        every one of the hexagons.

(2)   The main difference, if you use points of trisection, is that
        you get three interleaved sequences of hexagons rather
        than two. Again, in each sequence, the opposite sides of
        a hexagon tend to become parallel. Although, within each
        sequence, the hexagons get more like each other, there is
        not really a 'limiting hexagon'. You will have to take this
        on trust[1].

(3)   With a hexagon, you eventually get a line, which does not
        shrink to a point. If you start with an irregular pentagon,
        you eventaully get a pentagram. From a regular pentagon,
        you get a regular pentagon. Experiment with other initial
        figures, and with different rules for forming the nested
        polygon.

(4)   It turns out that the answer to (1) does hold for non-
        convex polygons. The general theory is elaborate: see the
        reference given in the footnote if you want a full and
        technical answer.

1 Or, if you are proficient in trigonometry, read the article by J.H.Cadwell, 'A property
of linear cyclic transformations', in the Mathematical Gazette, vol. 37, no. 320, p.85
(1953).

(5)   The current definitions are not adequate – for example, the first line of DIGIT.LIST will give a test outcome of TRUE for every non–negative number if the base is negative. In particular, if the input is zero, DIGIT.LIST will recurse until the space for keeping track of recursion is exhausted. While it is possible to make some changes so that DIGIT.LIST always gives some answer, the idea of a nega-tive base is not really sensible. The main snag is, what are digits? Can they be negative? Consider the number –16 in base –8. Is it represented as [– –2 0 [–8]] or as [2 0 [–8]]? The number 16 would be either [–2 0 [–8]] or [– 2 0 [–8]]. This means that either negative digits must be allowed, or that some apparently negative numbers are larger than some apparently positive ones. If you can live with these, fine...

(6)   Follow up the hint. To convert 3.74 to a base 8 form, keep multiplying by 8 until you get an integer, or you have multiplied by 8 four times. Convert the integer. Then move the decimal (or rather, octal) point leftward in the list the appropriate number of digits. Consider an example. The decimal number 3.74, would be written in base 8 as

      3.572702443650507534 12....

In decimal form, 3.74*8*8*8*8 is 15319.04...; rounding this to an integer gives 15319. Converting this to base 8 using CONVERT gives the list [3 5 7 2 7 [8]]. Shifting the point leftward four places gives a list [3 . 5 7 2 7 [8]]. Defining LOGO procedures to do all this is not too hard.

(7)   The snag, again, is deciding what is a digit or not. What is 2.6 in base 2.5? Obviously, it is just over [1 [2.5]], but how much over? You could apply the answer to exercise 6 here. There is a more serious snag. What is 100 in base 0.5? Think about this, and you will see the snag about digits much more clearly. In base 0.5, or any other base between 0 and 1, there is no such thing as a 'biggest digit'. Suppose there were, and that it was N. Then in base 0.5 the number NNN...NNN (however many times the digit N occurs) would be no bigger than

$$N * (1 + 0.5 + 0.25 + 0.125 + ...)$$

which is no bigger than

N / (1 - 0.5)

which is 2 * N. This means that you could not represent numbers bigger than this!

Index

Where an index item happens to be the main subject of several consecutive pages in the book, only the first of those pages is mentioned below. For example, Artificial Intelligence is the main theme on pages 8 and 9, so only page 8 is mentioned. There are no references below to items which are mentioned only in the appendices. This index is only intended to cover the main body of the book. Page references are given for the first appearance of the Terrapin LOGO procedures used in the examples. There is a separate index to the examples of LOGO procedures.

The following table tells you where to find the examples of LOGO procedures given in this book. Where several versions of a procedure were defined, a page number is given for each of them.